PASANELLA+KLEIN STOLZMAN+BERG

CONTEMPORARY
WORLD
ARCHITECTS

CAW

PASANELLA+KLEIN STOLZMAN+BERG

Preface by
Jayne Merkel

Foreword by
Walter Chatham

Introduction by
Richard Weinstein

Concept and Design by
Lucas H. Guerra
Oscar Riera Ojeda

This book is dedicated to
our friend and colleague
WAYNE BERG
July 15, 1946–February 25, 1999

ROCKPORT PUBLISHERS
GLOUCESTER, MASSACHUSETTS

First published in the United States of America by:
Rockport Publishers, Inc.
33 Commercial Street
Gloucester, Massachusetts 01930
Telephone: 978-282-9590
Fax: 978-283-2742

Distributed to the book trade and art trade in the United States of America by
North Light Books, an imprint of F & W Publications
1504 Dana Avenue
Cincinnati, Ohio 45207
Telephone: 513-531-2222

Other distribution by Rockport Publishers, Inc.

ISBN 1-56496-505-8
10 9 8 7 6 5 4 3 2 1
Manufactured in China.

Cover photograph: Reed Library Addition by Paul Warchol
Back cover photographs: (top) Art Collector's Apartment and (bottom) Root House Interior by Paul Warchol
Back flap photograph: (left to right) Wayne Berg, J. Arvid Klein, and Henry Stolzman by Kentaro Tsubaki
Pages 1–3 photograph: Root House Interior by Paul Warchol

Graphic Design: Lucas H. Guerra/Oscar Riera Ojeda
Layout: Oscar Riera Ojeda
Composition: Hunha Lee

CONTENTS

Preface by Jayne Merkel   6
Foreword by Walter Chatham   8
Introduction by Richard Weinstein   10

Public Buildings
Reed Library Addition and Renovation   16
Education and Development Center   26
Stabile Hall Dormitory   34
World War II Memorial   42
Williamsburg Community Center   48
Primary and Intermediate School 89M   54

Hotels
The Shoreham Hotel   60
The Franklin Hotel   68
The Mansfield Hotel   74

Residences
Art Collector's Apartment   84
Crafts Collector's Pied-à-Terre   98
Fifth Avenue Apartment   104
Prasada Apartment   110
Bachelor's Downtown Loft   114
The Root House   120

Appendix
Selected Buildings   136
List of Works and Credits   142
Acknowledgments   144

Preface

BY JAYNE MERKEL

Pasanella + Klein Stolzman + Berg may be unique among second-generation architecture firms for having developed a voice of its own consistent with that of its founding partners, yet attuned to the present. Henry Stolzman and Wayne Berg, who respectively joined Pasanella + Klein in 1978 and 1986 and became partners in 1986 and 1987, did not embrace the historically inspired postmodernism that many of their contemporaries adopted. They well could have; it was the prevailing trend when they began their careers. Columbia University, where Stolzman was trained, became one of its centers. And when Berg came to New York, he worked for Robert A. M. Stern Architects, which still practices post-modern classicism. Instead, like other architects their age who remained modernists, they rejected the purism of International Style modernism and accepted the importance of imagery, while remaining committed to modern materials and programs and to the spirit of their time. By the late '80s that spirit, influenced by post-modernism, was expressed with color, texture, and even some decorative detail. A respect for historical building fabric and a willingness to respond to the existing architectural conditions was taken for granted. In fact, the ability of Pasanella + Klein Stolzman + Berg to grasp the character of a place and preserve, respect, and enhance it may be its greatest strength, although the firm has always employed a spare modern architectural vocabulary, used new materials along with traditional ones, and combined modern open planning with traditional room arrangements.

The current firm's work continues the subtle, abstract, quietly of-the-moment modernism of Pasanella + Klein and maintains the earlier firm's respect for surrounding architectural features that was unusual for its time. Their dark-red-brick Little Italy apartments between Mott, Spring, and Elizabeth Streets in Manhattan—where an old school was demolished—fit into the streetscape so subtly that it is surprising to discover that 170 new housing units and a new, smaller school were constructed in the school's place. The new complex, while frankly modern and without the classicizing ornament of nearby dwellings, also has dark red brick, small double-hung windows, and street-level shops. Similarly, Pasanella + Klein Stolzman + Berg's Stabile Hall dormitory for Pratt Institute in Brooklyn takes its cues from surrounding buildings, which in this case differ considerably from one another. The dormitory, which steps back in deference to landmark faculty row houses across the street, recalls nearby industrial buildings on its upper stories and has a series of pavilions sheltering courtyards in the rear.

Giovanni Pasanella's Twin Parks housing complexes in the Bronx are by far the most overtly contextual of the schemes there designed by a number of well-known New York architects in the 1970s. Clad in the warm-toned brick of the neighborhood (though in larger blocks), Pasanella's buildings step up and down, forward and backward, responding to the lay of the land, nearby buildings, street patterns, and adjacent park landscapes. With similar sensitivity to its natural and architectural surroundings, Pasanella + Klein Stolzman + Berg's new academic building at the Clinch Valley campus of the University of Virginia at Wise reates and integrates a series of courtyards along the main pedestrian spine, which climbs at a gentle incline along the ridge of

a plateau. Responding both to its immediate neighbors and to the landscape of rolling Appalachian foothills, the building makes a connection, previously absent, between the ridge-top upper campus and the lower campus in the valley below.

When this book was being prepared in 1998, Berg, who had taught at Columbia University for the last several years and who was active in the New York architectural community, was the best-known designer in the firm. He led the firm's efforts on schools, campuses and institutional buildings. Working frequently on a large scale, as in the addition to Reed Library at the SUNY College at Fredonia, he was particularly adept at the interplay between building design and urban design. Stolzman concentrated mainly on hotel and residential projects, building on existing conditions and integrating new parts with original modern detail. But the partners critique one another's projects and work collaboratively with the various members of every design team. Arvid Klein, who serves as managing partner, holds the office together and provides historical continuity, wisdom and insight as well as architectural expertise.

The architects at Pasanella + Klein Stolzman + Berg continue to build on their firm's history in academic and institutional buildings. They design quietly luxurious apartments, usually for art collectors, as well as offices and commercial spaces and European-style hotels. Although very little publicly supported work in housing exists today in the United States, in 1997, the firm won a coveted commission, in an invitational competition, to design a community center at the Bauhaus-inspired Williamsburg Houses in Brooklyn and prevailed in the competition among a number of city's most prestigious architects to build a new dormitory for art and architecture students at Pratt Institute. The firm is a consistent winner in the annual AIA New York Chapter design awards competition, AIA New York State Excellence in Design awards competition, and awards programs in other states. In 1999, PKSB received the AIA New York Chapter Medal of Honor. Increasingly, the firm is a contender in a larger arena where its ability to articulate the character of a place and the experience of the contemporary condition quietly but convincingly is being recognized.

Views of the Fifth Avenue and Art Collector's Apartments, New York, New York (above left and right). Campus buildings at Clinch Valley College in Wise, Virginia and Pratt Institute in Brooklyn, New York (below left and right).

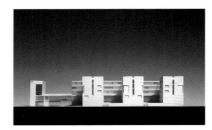

Foreword

BY WALTER CHATHAM

The firm of Pasanella + Klein Stolzman + Berg unites modern architecture and humanism to produce work that is crisp yet sensual. Building exteriors are abstractly composed yet evocative. Materials are used in a way that emphasizes the tactile contrast between opaque solids and light-transmitting planes. Inside, the architecture, furnishings, and decor work in harmony to create dynamic yet comfortable settings for the occupants.

Architecture today frequently suffers from an inability to reconcile intellectual rigor and stylishness. PKSB has managed to overcome this problem by embracing the seeming contradiction and treating each project as a unified whole. The abstract spatial and sculptural qualities inherent in the work ensure dynamic tension and excitement, but an underlying discipline prevents the arbitrary from ruining the effect. As a result, there is a feeling of inevitability about each project. No two are alike, and yet a common thread runs through them. History is neither deified nor denied. Rather, historic precedents are abstracted where appropriate in order to provide context and meaning to the work. Some of the work is romantic in feeling—the university buildings have an almost stark medieval cast to them and the firm's interiors have a pleasing theatrical quality. This is wholly consistent with a design philosophy that sees human use and enjoyment as the true goal for architecture. Great architecture creates a suitable backdrop for the drama played out within.

The artistic quality of PKSB's architecture is impeccable without being brash or obvious about it. PSKB's attitude toward design is fresh; it does not depend on formulaic solutions. Indeed, there is a "hipness" to the work more often characteristic of young, iconoclastic designers than of long-established architectural practices. It is rare to find the consistent attention to design and detail evident on the pages that follow. The fact that it has been produced by a firm is remarkable, as it is extremely difficult to maintain high standards within an organization. The studio system employed by PKSB is one key to the firm's success—the close collaboration of the talented partners is another. Uniting these factors is an underlying commitment to modern architecture in the heroic tradition, a commitment begun by Giovanni Pasanella and continued by J. Arvid Klein, Henry Stolzman, and Wayne Berg.

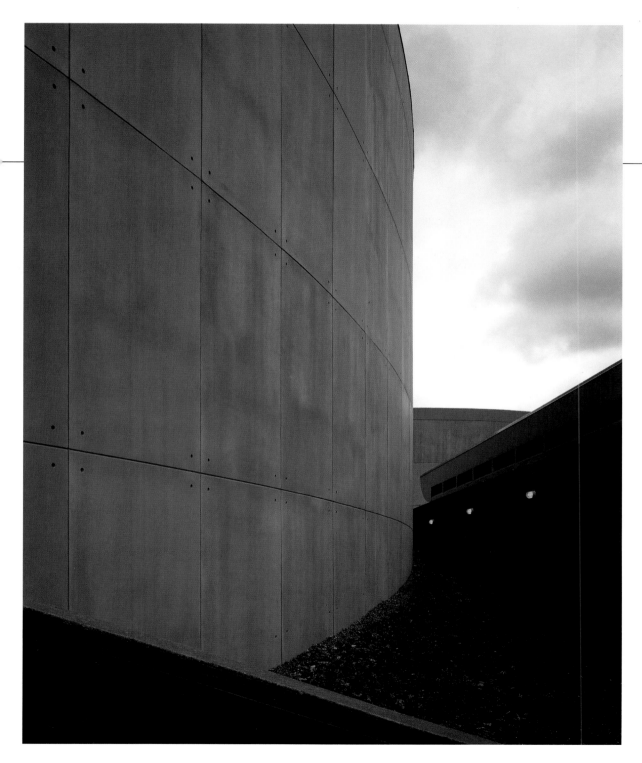

Inside the rare-book tower at Reed Library Addition, Fredonia, New York (below far left). Semi-transparent copper-mesh panels at the Root House, Ormond Beach, Florida (below left). The curved wall of Reed Library Addition alongside Pei & Partners' original concrete forms (left).

Introduction

BY RICHARD WEINSTEIN

We approach the millennium with architecture subject to the forces of entropy, with some practitioners employing theory (mostly from French sources) to invigorate their work, some finding their foundation in history, some—liberated from the module through the use of the computer—exploring non-Euclidean geometries. The variety of these approaches reflects the pluralistic trends within our political, social, and economic institutions. As we privatize experience through computers and television, we weaken the consensual values upon which a coherent architecture was based, especially when coherence was in the interests of a centralized establishment of power that promoted these values. Now these establishments operate mostly within the constraints established by democratic procedures and the complexities of global capitalism. Their power is consequently fragmented, and the value systems that once were a principal instrument of their influence are hopelessly weakened and confused.

Today architects are required to identify for themselves a set of institutional values upon which to base their work, and this leads them to certain clients with similar views. Not surprisingly, a process something like typecasting takes place, where architects are hired like character actors because their work is deemed appropriate for a certain kind of job. This encourages some architects to further differentiate their designs until there is no mistaking their personal signature. Carried to an extreme, this process resembles some of the grotesque results of natural selection noted by Darwin when he observed small birds with enormous beaks.

The origins of PKSB lie in the firm founded by Giovanni Pasanella in 1964. Programmatic invention, a base in humanist values, a strong formal presence, and attention to urban context characterized the office's work. The present character of the firm derived its direction from Arvid Klein, who became a partner in 1975 and maintained the values that continue to guide the work of the firm. Henry Stolzman, an early collaborator with both Pasanella and Klein, became a partner in 1986, and Wayne Berg became a partner in 1987. The more recent work of PKSB has now come into its own and has received substantial recognition in the form of awards and significant commissions. Because there has been a continuity of values underlying the work of the office—in contrast to the disruption of commitment experienced by the profession at large—we would do well to understand the interaction between the projects, their aesthetic, and these values.

The humanist position in architecture today is best understood as placing the highest value on each space serving its purpose without being compromised by overriding abstract formal intentions. Pursuing such an approach requires the separate analysis of each component, to determine how light, scale, and configuration may impact the character of the space. Differences are further enhanced by materials and detailing strategies. It follows that to proceed in this way it is necessary to have an idea of what the character of that space should be to support the activity for which it was designed.

This approach is evident in the key drawings—exploded axonometrics—that accompany the three largest and most ambitious projects to date: the library addition at Fredonia, the college at University of Virginia, and the residence hall at Pratt. In each case the separate components of the design are given their own identities as they float in axonometric space—a clue to how they were originally analyzed as independent entities. This way of conceptualizing a design also promotes a close analysis of program that sometimes leads to innovation like the shared studio homework spaces in the Pratt project. These efforts to promote community through opportunities for interaction are a recurring theme in all the public projects.

Programmatic innovations are also promoted by compositional necessities that occur after the primary analysis is completed. The formal issues presented by the design method outlined above occur when the separate components are organized with respect to the visual discipline of the whole. It then becomes necessary to modify and inflect the parts to achieve a balance between their surviving identity and an aspiration for the coherence of the whole. For this to be accomplished at Pratt, a gallery and artist-in-residence block was invented to anchor the massing of the front elevation at the right. This invention also works to frame and emphasize the main entrance and student lounge.

A further extension of the humanist position in architecture is sensitivity to contextual issues, evident in the early buildings by Pasanella in the Bronx. Over time, this sensitivity has become sophisticated under the pressure of increasingly complicated programs, until it has become a principal determinant of form and is even embraced as an opportunity to establish scale relationships with adjacent buildings and to give purpose to site planning decisions. The major formal moves in the Pratt building are in response to surrounding site conditions, and each of the larger projects cannot be understood except as a resolution of programmatic intent and external vectors. Attention to context can be understood as an effort to secure a continuity of cultural values. The effort required to achieve this connection through contemporary formal devices, rather than through glib historical reference, gives these values greater purchase on the future.

The completed image of the buildings achieves a tense balance between the differentiation of the parts and the accommodation of the whole to its program and context. Differentiation is achieved by changes in materials, the use of transparencies and layering, and by the permeability of the mass at the ground plane with large openings. Together these visual strategies produce a metaphor of individual self-determination in anxious balance with binding social forces, demonstrating an engagement with a central cultural issue of our moment in history. These themes are advanced with equal or even greater success at the Clinch Valley campus of the University of Virginia, which enjoys a masterful harmony of proportion that gives the work an appropriate serenity of aspect. Pratt is the much tougher project, in Brooklyn, with very little bucolic about it. One might notice in the rather ominous juxtaposition of the

Rendering, World War II Memorial design for Washington, D.C. (above far left). Building entrances, Reed Library, Fredonia, New York (above left) and Education and Development Center at Clinch Valley College, Wise, Virginia (above right).

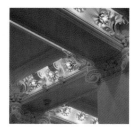

three housing blocks against the diaphanous curtain wall, a reminiscence of the much earlier Gallatin County Detention Center (no diaphanous anything here). The belligerent, hulking physiognomy of Berg's remarkable early work reminds us of the existence in his work of powerful subterranean forces, however much they are overlaid with humane intent, gracious proportions, and a lyric eye for felicitous detail. There is a brooding power in the massing of volumes and an effort in the later projects to undermine the continuity of elevations with large openings. Both Virginia and Pratt exhibit this ambiguous tendency, which adds depth and complexity of meaning.

A splendid eye for detail on a smaller scale characterizes the apartment for an art collector. Notice how the lighting system and its track become a series of moldings that frame the spaces of the rooms. This aesthetic, which approaches minimalism in its choice of materials and their handling, is shared by Henry Stolzman, who is chiefly responsible for the small hotels the firm has designed. They are understated, atmospheric, and sensual. While Berg acts as a collegial critic of Stolzman's design, Klein sees his role as advocating the interests of the client, and Stolzman in turn adopts the role of a critic for Berg's work. These interactions account for the sympathetic relation between all the projects done by PKSB, from the large buildings to the canopied bed in an intimate hotel. One senses in the details and choices of materials the same discipline that is applied to the composition of the large elevations and the inflections of their plans.

At first reading, there is a grace and simplicity in the work on all scales, overriding the complexity of subsequent readings. It is as if everything begins with a kind of managed chaos, because everything is initially considered to have an equal claim on the outcome. These claims are then submitted to unsentimental analysis and subordinated to an emerging purpose—when that purpose is finally felt to encompass a proper adjustment of competing parts to a satisfactory whole. Issues of program, context, budget, proportion, structure, systems, and formal invention are initially in competition and conflict to be tamed and, to a degree, are calmed by the process of design. In contrast, work at the extremes of architecture, with few exceptions, achieves formal surprise at the expense of almost everything else that buildings are supposed (by most of the world) to do.

At a moment of architectural extremes—from the theft of history to the appropriation of the latest science and philosophy, from the exploration of formal invention enabled by the computer to the sentiments of green architecture—here is an architecture that holds the center without compromising the modern project. And in holding the center, PKSB asserts the enduring value of an architecture that will not sacrifice one component of the design process to achieve notoriety with another. Instead, the analytic, the contextual, the tectonic, materiality and proportion, the discipline of mind, and the pleasure of convincing form—all seek to remain in balance. But the balance is achieved out of our moment, with its uncertainties, anxieties, and changing values expressed in the work and at the same time finding comfort in the continuity of the humanist tradition.

Lighting fixtures for the Crafts Collector's Pied-à-Terre, New York, New York (above left) and for the Mansfield Hotel, New York, New York (above right). Steel-framed glass doors enclose the terrace of the Art Collector's Apartment, New York, New York (left).

Public Buildings ▶

Reed Library Addition and Renovation

STATE UNIVERSITY OF NEW YORK AT FREDONIA

Designing an addition to Reed Library, the architects felt at first, was like "being asked to add onto the Parthenon." Though the original library was only one story high, it was a massive story, with superscaled windows in deep protruding frames. The heavy poured-in-place and precast concrete monolith was one of five I. M. Pei & Partners structures set down in the middle of a modest brick teacher's college campus in the 1960s, like Stonehenge slabs in a field. The only possible way to approach it was by contrast—with a collection of strong (but smaller) geometric volumes grouped to one side. A sweeping precast concrete wall, matching the original perfectly, curves away from the existing blank south wall. The west side of this arc-shaped section is glazed and, at night, casts light out to the campus. Its grid of windows, set in a deep aluminum frame, encloses a stair atrium which creates a courtyard with the other library components. Also facing into the courtyard is a concrete block cylinder housing the rare book collection. A modestly-scaled, new five-story brick rectangle filled with books and study carrels completes the composition of geometric solids. This simple bar, the addition's south façade, is pierced with a grand entry archway that leads to the main library entry. Together, the new structures that comprise the addition create a ground floor pedestrian passageway from the south campus's older dormitory quadrangles to the central 1960s campus, where a triangular second-level walkway ties Pei's library to his student union, art center, and administration building.

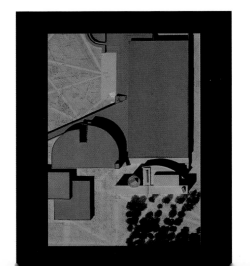

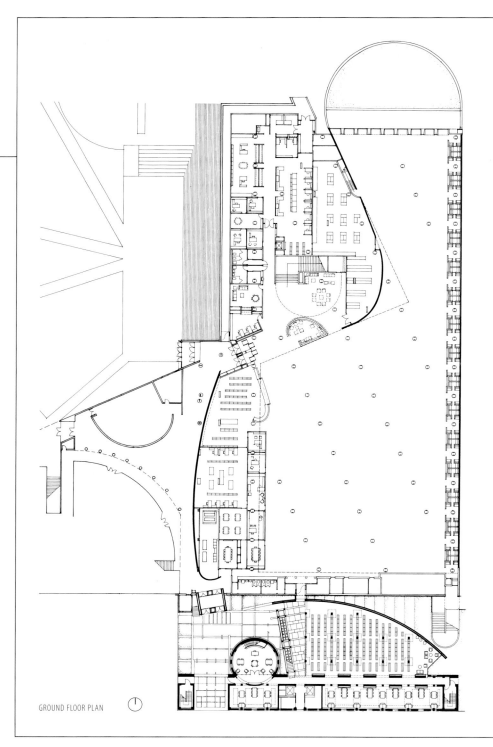

The four-story addition is attached
to the south end of the existing
single-story library, where it creates a
new courtyard with adjacent buildings.
The sweep of the addition's curved,
concrete wall is the backdrop to Pei &
Partners' original building and defines
the edge of the central campus.

GROUND FLOOR PLAN

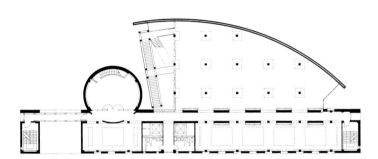

THIRD FLOOR PLAN

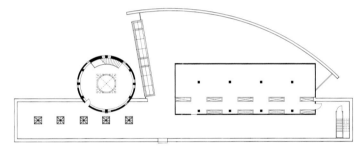

FIFTH FLOOR PLAN

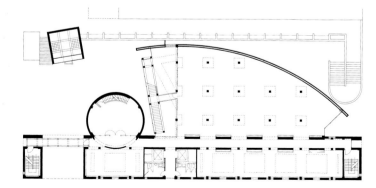

SECOND FLOOR PLAN

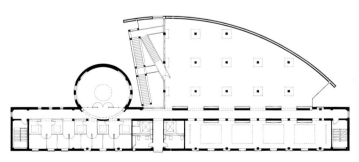

FOURTH FLOOR PLAN

The new entry sequence reinforces the bond between the original building and its addition. The arch, cut into the addition's brick bar, guides visitors toward the original library's new entry pavilion. This procession turns a back door that had become the library's de facto main entrance into its formal one.

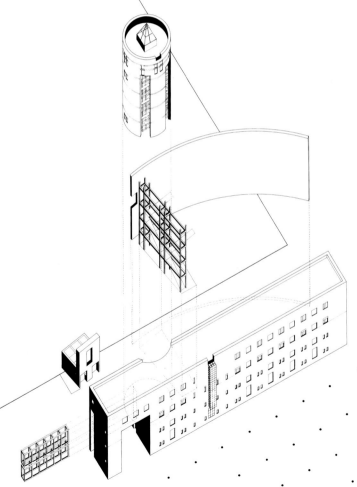

The addition's glass atrium is its vertical circulation core. Clearly visible from the outside, the atrium's network of stair-cases and structural poured-in-place concrete members enlivens the building. Book stacks are screened from the atrium by a translucent panel wall.

Education and Development Center

This long, narrow classroom building runs along the ridge of a 50-foot- (15-meter-) high plateau, creating a visual image where none existed before and connecting two plain, existing modern academic buildings. It also ties together the upper and lower campuses of this small scattered Appalachian college by means of a walkway from the de facto entry at a parking lot on the north to the ceremonial campus gates on the south. The new 30,000-square-foot (2,800-square-meter) Education and Development Center even creates ties between the four academic departments located there, because the classrooms, laboratories, and faculty offices are distributed throughout several levels around vertical circulation nodes to discourage the formation of departmental ghettoes.

The carefully composed east façade creates a formal courtyard for the upper campus, with the new building's main entry as its focal point. Passing through this space, the new campus-wide pedestrian promenade provides wheelchair access to all the buildings of the upper campus, where a planned science building will eventually enclose the quad. On the opposite side, the building's less formal, more freely drawn west façade looks out over the lower campus and into the Appalachian foothills. Art studios, located on the lower level, open directly to the outside, so that classes can move outdoors to work in small groups on the hilltop. Seen from the lower campus below, this side of the building operates boldly and at a large scale, relating to the mountains that ring the campus. The project received a citation in the 43rd Annual *Progressive Architecture* awards competition of 1996, the month before the magazine ceased publication.

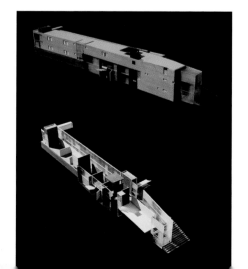

The west façade steps down to meet the steep grade of the descending hill, creating large, loft-like art studio spaces in the building's midsection. The more opaque northern end of the main bar contains media rooms outfitted for presentations and distance learning. The southern end's stairwells and science labs connect by bridge to the campus's main science building.

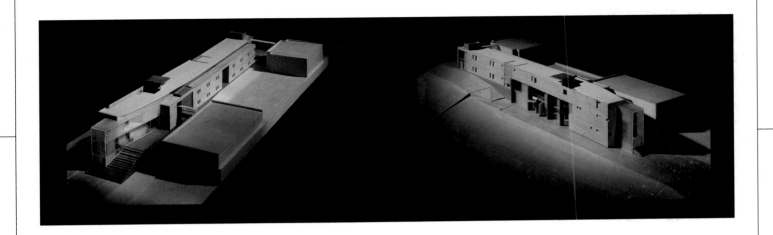

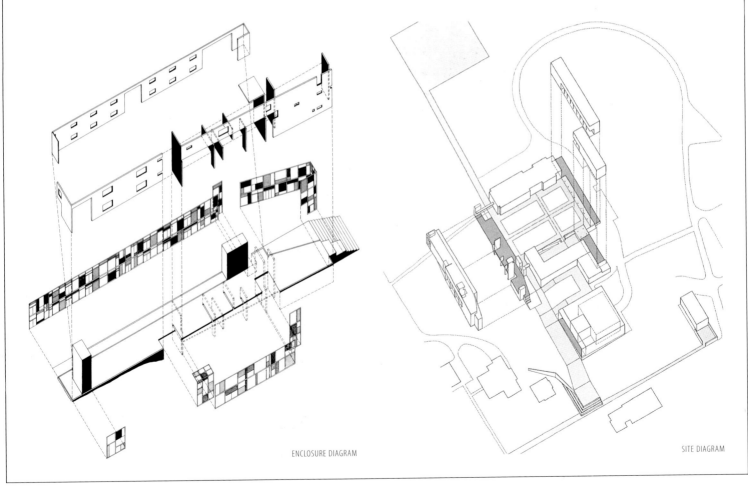

ENCLOSURE DIAGRAM

SITE DIAGRAM

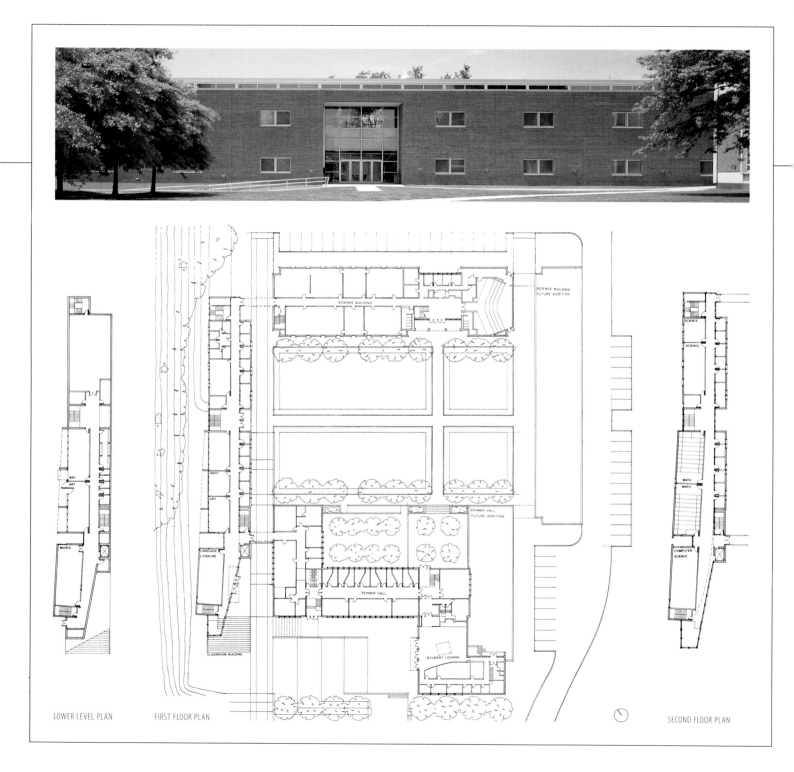

LOWER LEVEL PLAN   FIRST FLOOR PLAN   SECOND FLOOR PLAN

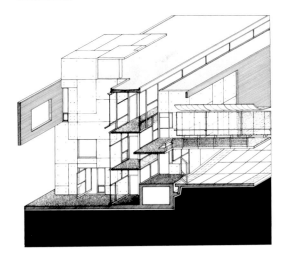

BUILDING SECTION

The Center houses computer labs, traditional and electronic classrooms, art studios, and a media center with a television production room. Each department is stacked around a vertical circulation node, with points of spatial overlap and transparency allowing views from one department to another. Interior materials are simple, easy to maintain, and industrial in character.

Stabile Hall Dormitory

PRATT INSTITUTE, BROOKLYN, NEW YORK

Forming the eastern edge of the Institute's five-block-long urban campus in a transitional area outside the gated, tree-filled yard, this dormitory separates a row of landmark faculty town houses from a parking lot. The long, low, bar-like west façade faces the street with a two-story brick band, capped with an aluminum canopy and penetrated with small square windows to emphasize its domestic scale. Then it steps back where it is sheathed with an aluminum and glass curtain wall like those on industrial buildings nearby and rises three more stories. On the east side, the bar divides into three five-story pavilions with rooms oriented to the courtyards created between them.

Commissioned in an invitational competition for a dormitory specifically for architecture and design students, the building provides living, social, and work space for 240 freshmen. Students enter the building through a porte-cochere and pass by lounges on their way to their own rooms. Views into these glass-enclosed, semi-public lounge spaces, half of which are equipped as studios for art and architecture, show the social and work activity within, encouraging discussion and collaboration on works in progress. Because these double-height working lounges are shared by two floors, they offer opportunities for students to interact with those whose living quarters are a level above or below.

An unusual addition to the dormitory's program is the large gallery above the main entrance in the prow of the building, where students can curate and mount exhibits or host artists-in-residence, connecting themselves to the campus and the larger art world.

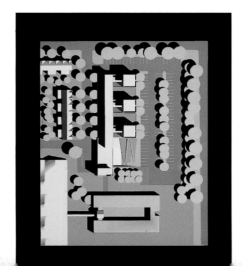

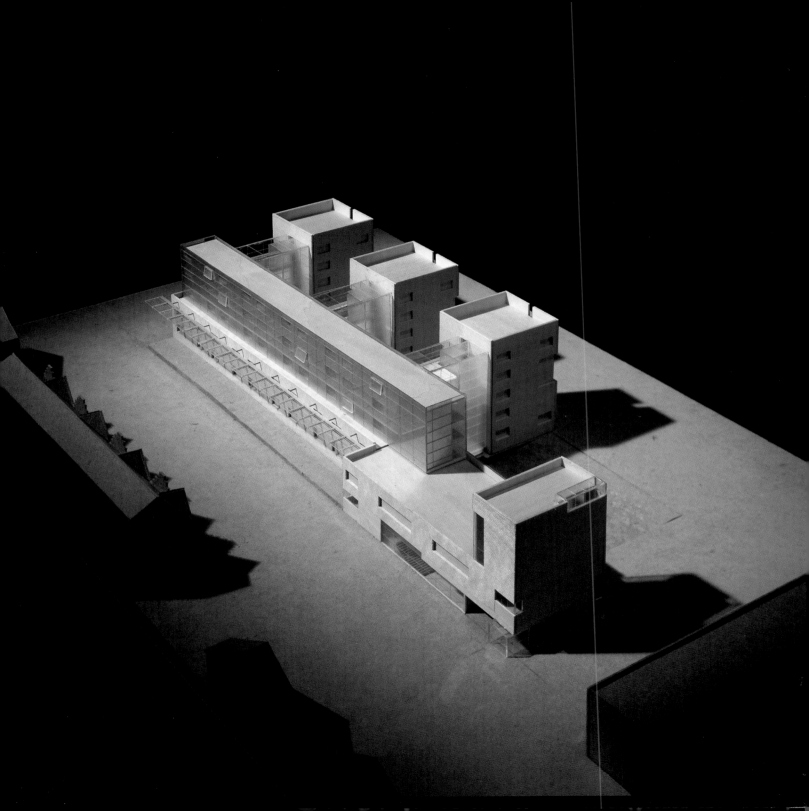

Stabile's brick lower bar reflects the scale and texture of the landmark Pratt Row faculty houses it faces across Emerson Place. In the townhouse tradition, the first floor of the two-story bar is raised three feet (one meter) from grade, so that residents' windows are just above pedestrian eye level and thus remain private. The windows look out over a landscape band that buffers them from the street.

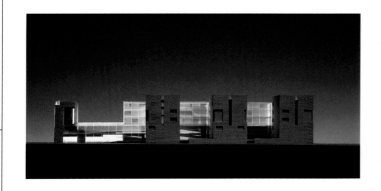
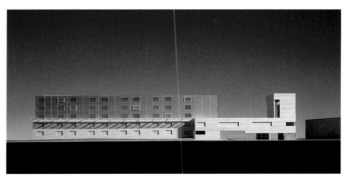

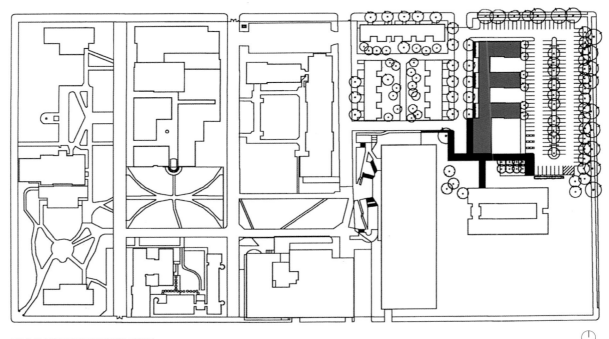

SITE PLAN AND VARIOUS LAYOUT UNIT OPTIONS

Stabile Hall Dormitory

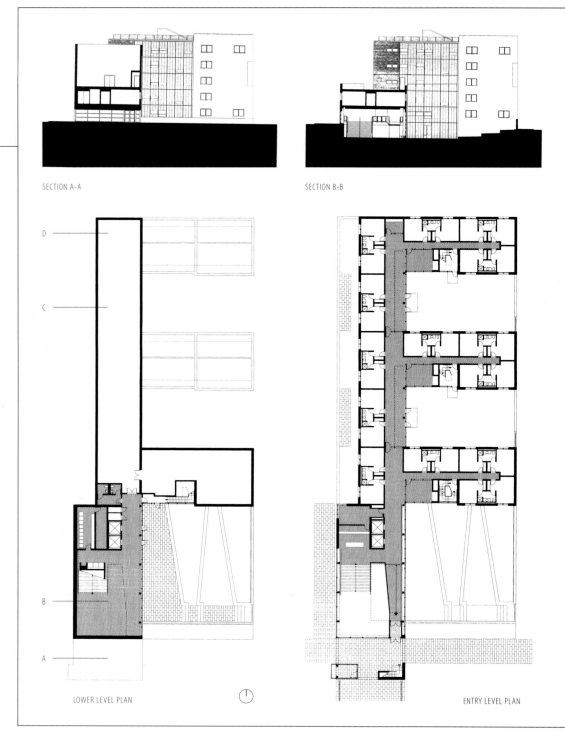

SECTION A-A

SECTION B-B

D

C

B

A

LOWER LEVEL PLAN

ENTRY LEVEL PLAN

As a dormitory for art students, the building is designed to integrate the everyday activities of living and producing artwork. Distributed throughout the residence hall, studio-like "homework spaces" provide room for larger, messier projects and collaborative work. These double-height spaces are shared by clusters of rooms on two floors, encouraging residents to mix beyond their usual groups of floormates.

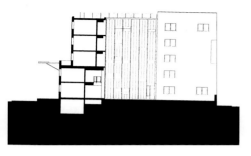

SECTION C-C

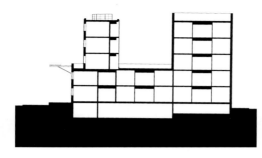

SECTION D-D

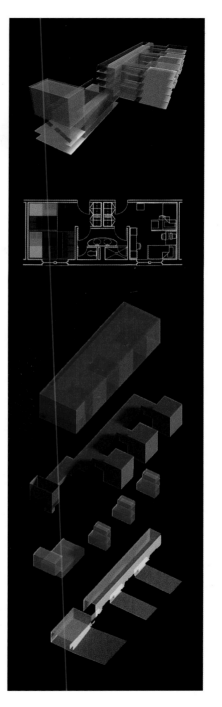

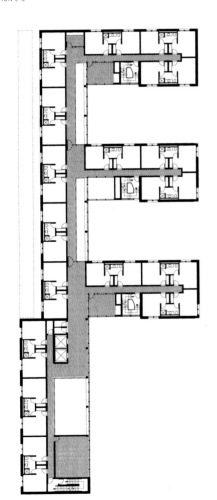

SECOND LEVEL PLAN

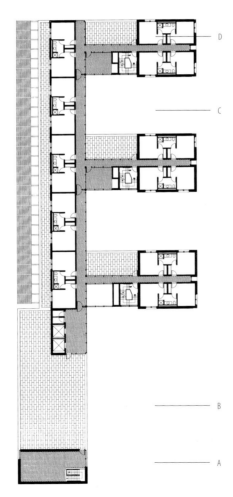

D

C

B

A

THIRD-FIFTH LEVEL PLAN

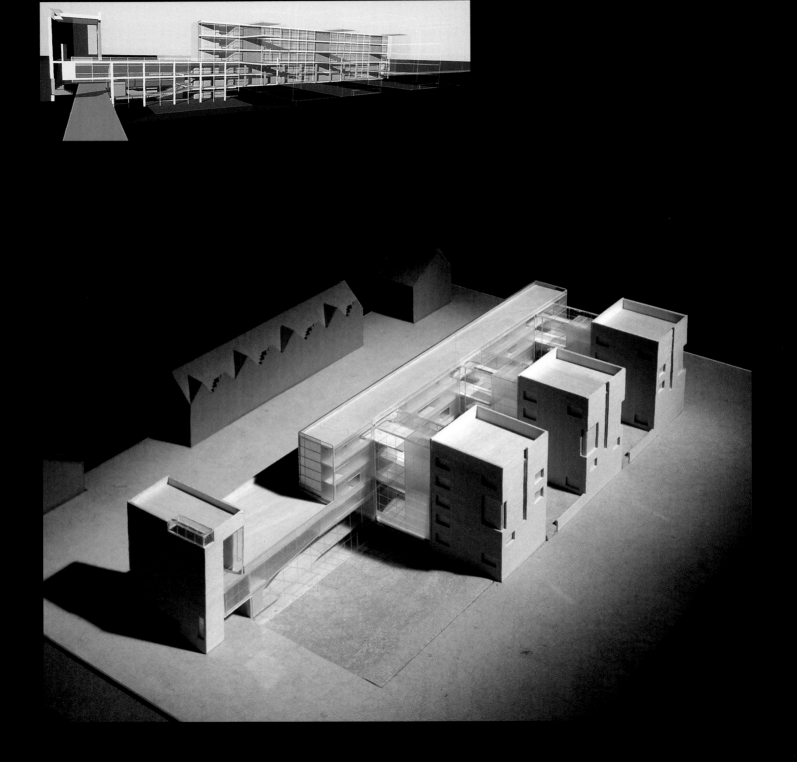

World War II Memorial

Since memorials today commemorate quietly the many citizens who have given their lives for a cause, rather than celebrate a few solitary heroes, the architects were able to preserve the public character of the site of the World War II Memorial at the Rainbow Pool on axis with the Lincoln and Washington Monuments in the middle of the Washington Mall. The pool became a symbolic ocean separating the Atlantic and Pacific theaters surrounded by a rotunda rising only as high as the existing trees and the bases of the Washington and Lincoln Memorials. The outer walls of the rotunda are made of limestone, the material of Washington D.C., and inner walls are steel, the material of war. Light passes through the inner walls and into the rotunda's stair-filled interior through the names of the war dead incised in the metal surface.

The rebuilt Rainbow Pool is paved with glass blocks, etched with the names of famous battles, and gridded with water columns spraying mist. A place of silence, light and rainbows, the pool can be occupied only by the spirit and elements of nature. Visitors to the memorial can walk around and under it. The flags of the four principal Allied nations trace its edge; entrances, one for each of the four freedoms, are at its corners. The Hall of Memory and the World War II Museum are buried beneath the glass-bottomed pool, where their interiors are bathed in natural light, filtered through water and shadows.

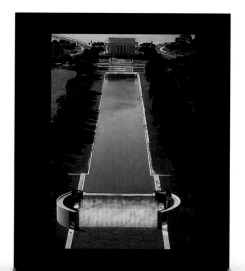

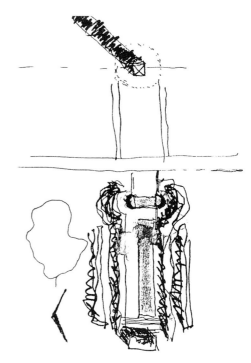

From a distance, the memorial's curved walls appear solid and impermeable. In fact, they are buildings visitors may enter, and their inner steel walls are penetrable by light. The Hall of Memory and World War II Museum, which lie beneath the glass-bottomed reflecting pool, join the two buildings.

42'-3 1/4"

Public Path / connects with Mall Path System
leads to Place of Rainbows & Hall of Memory & Museum
(Also connects to Halls of Names

Area of Museum Below
56882 S.F.

Wall Building/
Stone
Contains Halls of Names
Defignes Place of Rainbows

Rainbow Pool / Glass Block
Bottom lets light down to Hall of Memories Below
- Battle Names Etched in Glass pool
Shadows floor of hall below

Flag poles / U.S.A.
or Big 4 Allies

(Metal Wall with Names
cut thru - lights space &
allows view of Rainbows
as a perforated scrim -
Shadows of people
visable to outdoor room
Below

168'-9"

Glass Roof over
Place of Rainbows

Elevator

Spray Mist Water Columns/ Cast Rainbows thru
Silent space occupied by memory & Light

Tower of 4 Freedoms
(Stair to hall of Names)

Private Path - of pilgramage & Remberence
(loops thru 4 Freedpm Towers & Halls of Names)

Pool aligns with existing Reflecting Pool

CONCEPT SITE PLAN

1"=50'

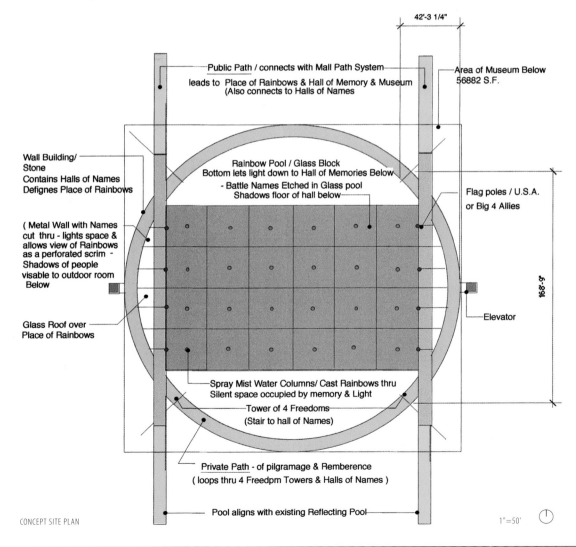

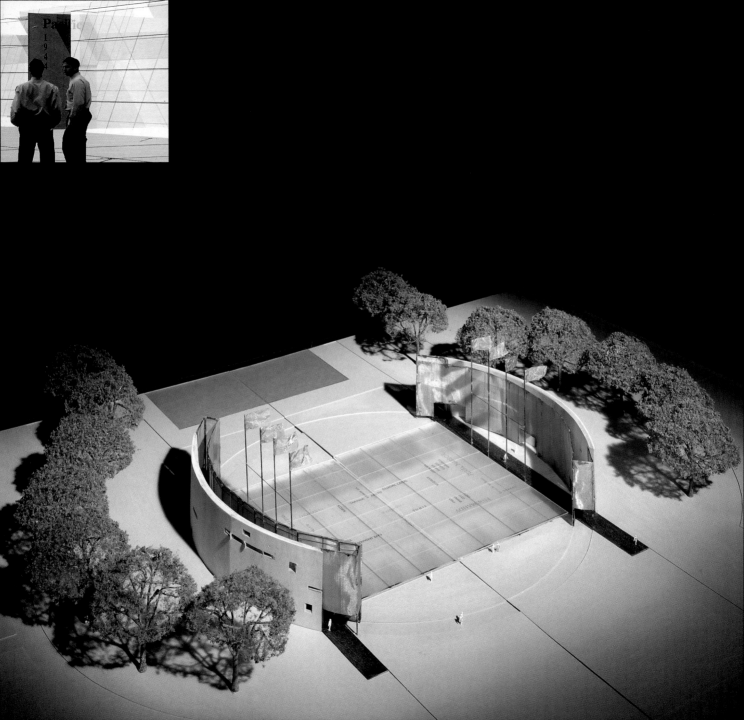

Williamsburg Community Center

BROOKLYN, NEW YORK

Chain-link fences, which surround an asphalt-paved park and define the ball courts and playgrounds inside, inspired the Williamsburg Community Center, though the architects who designed the long, low, flat-roofed Williamsburg houses in 1937 were inspired by their European colleagues who had built the first International Style housing blocks a decade earlier.

The chain-link fence is both means and metaphor for this building, where security is a concern of the neighborhood residents who will use the building and of the New York City Housing Authority officials who were building community centers at housing projects throughout the city in the late 1990s. The idea was to fill barren plazas with buildings and direct youthful energies into sports and arts.

A plaza was not the problem in Williamsburg, where horizontal housing blocks set diagonally to the street grid fill most of the site. The Center was to be located in the park, where chain-link provided a sense of enclosure and views of the activities taking place there. So that the Center may become part of the park, its walls are composed of a series of reinforced glass garage and airplane-hangar doors, which open to combine interior and exterior space. These transparent, flexible interior walls make it possible to close off some spaces when only a few are in use and also offer views and overlaps from one activity area to another, creating a sense of community involvement in shared activities.

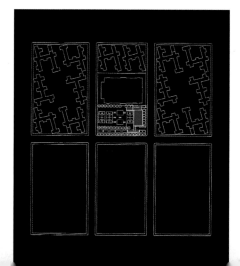

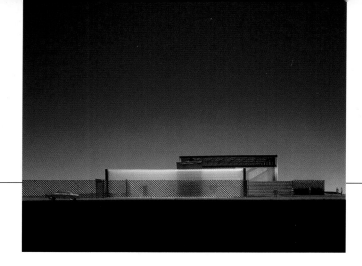

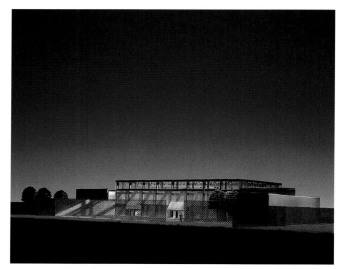

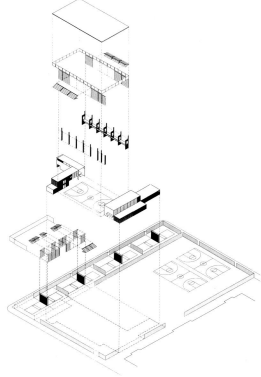

Breaking down its large mass, the building comprises a series of small pavilions scaled to the playground and organized by function. The Center's varied program includes gyms and locker rooms, classrooms, a movie projection booth, darkrooms, studios, and multipurpose space.

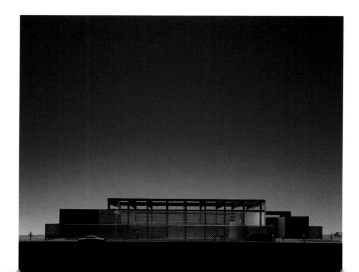

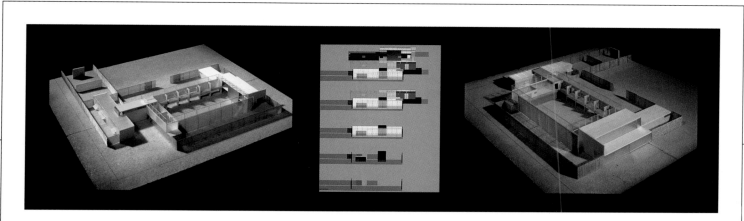

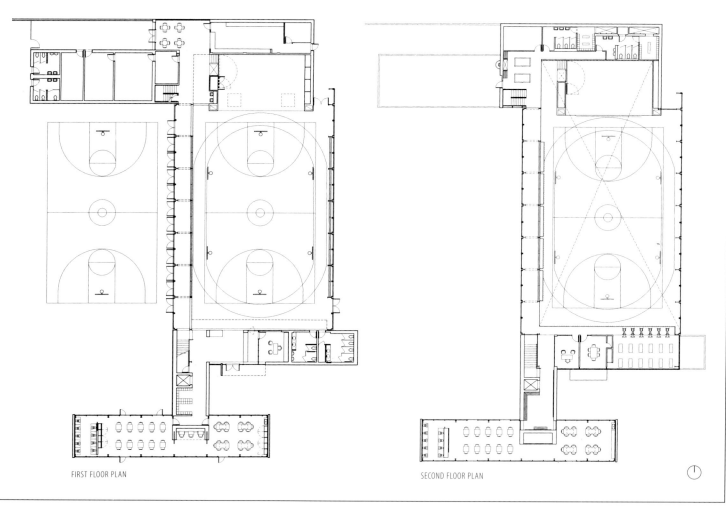

FIRST FLOOR PLAN

SECOND FLOOR PLAN

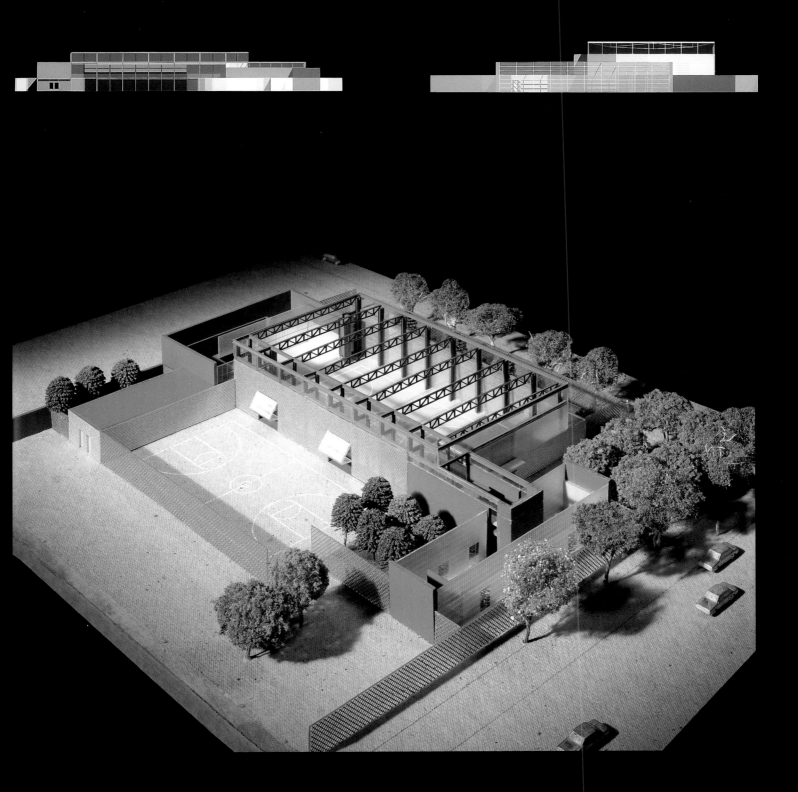

Primary and Intermediate School 89M

BATTERY PARK CITY, NEW YORK CITY

While nestled at the base of a new apartment tower, this school's design is everywhere influenced by the Lower Manhattan cityscape. Big windows offer views of the Statue of Liberty and Wall Street skyscrapers. Bends in its wide-open corridors reflect the winding streets of the seventeenth-century city responsible for its trapezoidal site. And in true urban fashion, the tall, well-lit corridors approximate city streets themselves. Besides having twists and turns, the halls contain space for planned meetings and chance conversation, storefront-like windows into classrooms, and entrances to more public places like the cafeteria, auditorium, and gym.

Like most of Manhattan, the 800-student school extends upward rather than outward, with an auditorium on top of the cafeteria, a gymnasium on top of the auditorium, and an open courtyard visible from the apartments above. The courtyard lights the library on one side, the corridor on the other, and it offers opportunities for urban gardening and science experiments in this city-kids' school which serves loft dwellers of Tribeca and residents of the post-modern high-rise "new town in town," Battery Park City. Classrooms for older children are located on the upper floors of the five-story structure. When students at PS/IS 89M pass to another grade, they will literally go up.

The school's most public areas—the auditorium and gym, for example—may be used by groups after hours. These heavily used, multipurpose areas are concentrated on the ground floor and in the "activity core" that runs up the center of the building. The fifth floor has an additional multipurpose space: a courtyard that is open to the sky. The courtyard's glazed walls spill natural light into the library on one side and the main circulation corridor on the other.

FIRST FLOOR PLAN

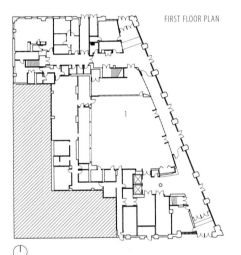

1

SECOND FLOOR PLAN

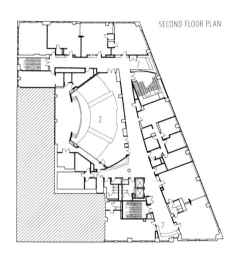

2

7

THIRD FLOOR PLAN

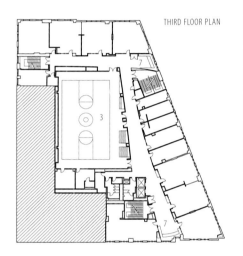

3

7

7

FOURTH FLOOR PLAN

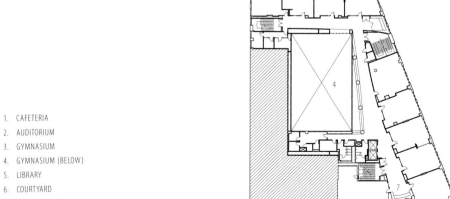

4

7

7

FIFTH FLOOR PLAN

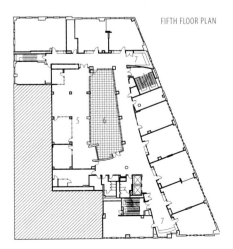

5

7

7

1. CAFETERIA
2. AUDITORIUM
3. GYMNASIUM
4. GYMNASIUM (BELOW)
5. LIBRARY
6. COURTYARD
7. MULTIPURPOSE

Hotels ▶

The Shoreham Hotel

33 WEST 55TH STREET, NEW YORK, NEW YORK

The allusions to the Shoreham's Art Deco past are so subtle and exacting that the hotel has more of the snappy urbane spirit of New York in the 1920s than it would have had if the lost detailing had been restored, as the owners had originally intended. The original overscaled marquee has been replaced by a new, tilted, steel-and-glass canopy, with metal mesh draperies flowing over sconces on each side. Inside, the past lives on in original Warren McArthur tubular steel tables and chairs, Winold Reiss murals in the lobby and lounge, and framed black-and-white Karl Blossfeldt photogravures throughout the hotel. But the airplane wing reception desk, the wavy ceiling overhead, the vaulted silver leaf canopy hiding pipes, and the gunmetal paneling masking columns in the lounge are obviously of our own time, without reference to any particular modern period. Similarly, the thin glass-and-steel doors, delicate geometric metal tables, lamps, and benches, and backlit perforated steel headboards in the relatively small guest rooms seem to belong there because they are exactly the right scale, with a lightness and elegance that comforts and dazzles as the same time. Like PKSB's other hotels for the Gotham Hospitality Group, the place has a domestic European "small hotel" ambience because of the delicate touch and attention to detail.

The Shoreham's exterior and lobby before renovation.

The original low marquee was replaced with a two-story opening in the limestone which locates the understated, asymmetrical entry at the building's center. The boutique hotel can never be confused with the larger hotel at the corner.

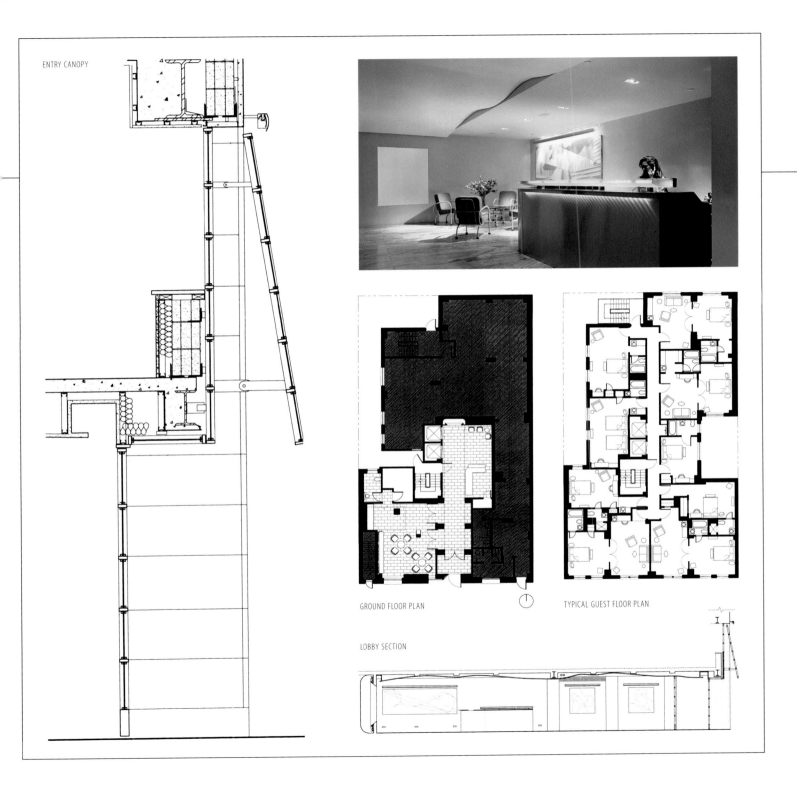

ENTRY CANOPY

GROUND FLOOR PLAN

TYPICAL GUEST FLOOR PLAN

LOBBY SECTION

The Shoreham Hotel

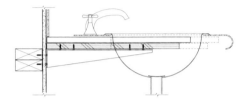

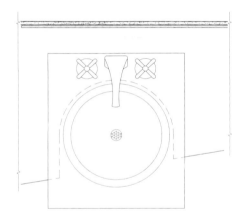

Attention to detail extends throughout the project. The reception desk's writing surface is illuminated cast resin, which is also used for the light fixtures in the passenger elevators and the backlit vases at each floor lobby.

VANITY DETAIL

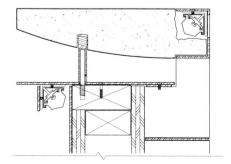

RECEPTION DESK DETAIL

In the suites, sandblasted steel and opaline glass doors provide privacy between the rooms without sacrificing the flow of the spaces or blocking the passage of natural light. As in the public areas, custom furniture pieces conserve space and bring unexpected touches to everyday objects.

The Franklin Hotel

184 EAST 87TH STREET, NEW YORK, NEW YORK

Few aesthetic clues existed for the conversion of this shabby single-room occupancy hotel into this European style "small hotel." All the building had going for it was its location on a pleasant block on the posh Upper East Side of Manhattan, but the transformation was nothing short of magical, as the budget was only $1.5 million for the nine-story, 13,500 square-foot (1,250-square-meter) building with fifty-one guest rooms as well as public spaces which also needed redecoration. And the rooms measure only 100–153 square feet (10–14 square meters). But curved tabletops, desks, and dressers save space; clouds of fabric suspended from ceiling-mounted steel rods over each bed add drama without clutter or major expense; furniture is made of handsome but inexpensive cherry plywood simply cut into planes so that no joinery is required; steel frames are sandblasted so that welded joints become part of the textured aesthetic.

Although the lobby is small, marble slabs on steel frames create a handsome and stylish reception desk and lounge buffet; fresh flowers and original works of art add character. A bench along one wall and buffet lining the other maximize the space in the breakfast room, where frosted glass set in metal frames scaled to the furniture brings in light from an open space in the rear and an Art Nouveau statue of Diana on a tall pedestal turns the opening into a charming niche.

The Franklin's exterior and lobby before renovation

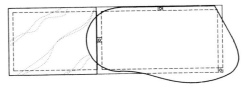

RECEPTION DESK DETAIL

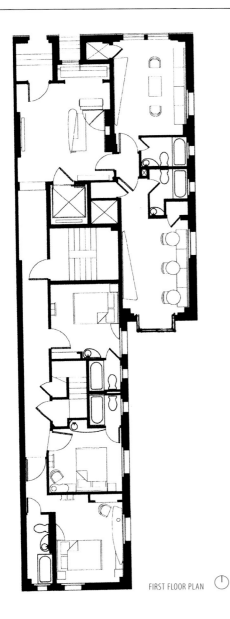

FIRST FLOOR PLAN

Public spaces were inserted into the original ground-floor plan, achieving an unusually intimate scale for an urban hotel. The breakfast room, lobby, video library, corridors and the guestrooms share materials and design motifs, maintaining a consistent design language throughout public and private zones (left, opposite page and previous spread, right).

To minimize costs, simple sheets of cherry plywood were used in a straightforward manner that required little craftsmanship. At the bedside, the plywood was cut into curved shapes to form desktops, while in the corridors, large sheets were used as backing for supporting shelves and display mirrors. In the smallest rooms, where built-in closets could not be accommodated, full-length mirrors were mounted on plywood and set out from the wall to conceal the hang rod.

The Mansfield Hotel

12 WEST 44TH STREET, NEW YORK, NEW YORK

When they started to peel away numerous successive "modernizations" of the turn-of-the-century Mansfield Bachelor Apartments, the architects had no idea they would find a skylighted dome in the shell of an old Irish pub on the ground floor or elaborate coffered ceilings in the lobby. And the owners had no idea the architects would cleverly replace the missing glass panes with affordable transparent steel mesh or light the florid coffers so that they glow from within. No one knew that when they stripped layers of paint from the bays over the rusticated Beaux Arts base they would find copper to give the facade a golden glow. Where no historic detailing remained, they added compatible new features, like the pilasters and wall paneling in the lobby and ebony-stained bookcases in the old bar, now a clubby library where breakfasts and desserts are served and concerts take place from time to time.

An old marble staircase next to the elevator bank was restored. New custom-designed furniture in the 131 guest rooms and suites recalls the past in a modern way—with sleek granite bathrooms, etched glass sconces and paneled doors, and iron and wire-mesh sleigh beds. Old things made inventively new enable this modestly-priced, 12-story, 50,000-square-foot (4,650-square-meter) gem, *Interiors* magazine's "Best Hotel" of 1996, to take its place proudly on the same block with some of the grandest old clubs and hotels in New York.

The Mansfield's exterior and lobby before renovation

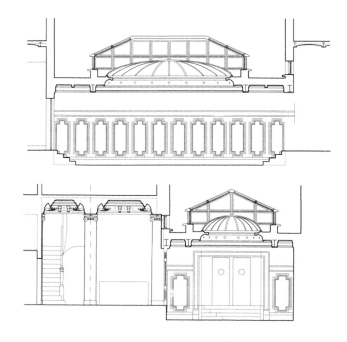

In addition to the reception lobby, the main floor contains a breakfast lounge and library. Where possible, original architectural details were restored; where necessary, they were replicated, and when feasible, reinterpreted (this and opposite page).

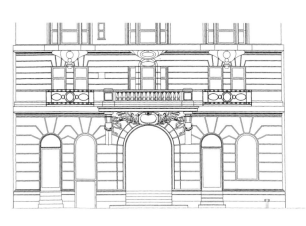

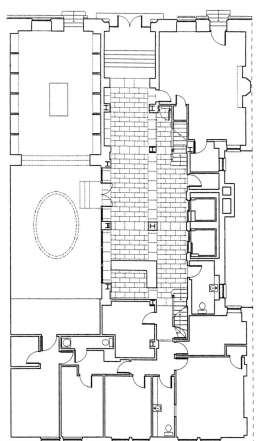

ENTRY FLOOR PLAN

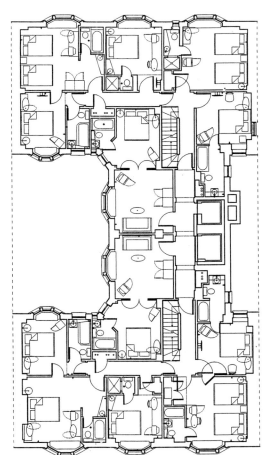

TYPICAL FLOOR PLAN

Art Deco antiques from the Philippines, period paintings, newly commissioned etched-glass doors, and custom designed furniture blend with the original architectural details, which are ebonized to reflect a more modern sensibility. The duplex penthouse was carved out of a former storeroom.

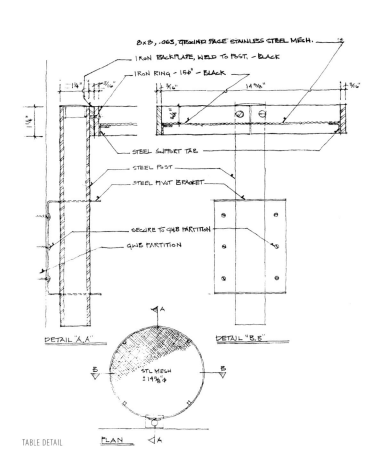

8×8, .063, GROUND FACE STAINLESS STEEL MESH.

IRON BACKPLATE, WELD TO POST. - BLACK

IRON RING - 15½" - BLACK

STEEL SUPPORT TAB

STEEL POST

STEEL PIVOT BRACKET

SECURE TO GWB PARTITION

GWB PARTITION

DETAIL "A,A"

DETAIL "B,B"

STL MESH
± 14⅝" Φ

PLAN

TABLE DETAIL

Typical rooms are not the standard at the Mansfield. The penthouse suite has a sleeping loft overlooking the double-height living room. Suites come in many configurations, each of which emphasizes the available architectural elements from its previous life.

Residences ▶

Art Collector's Apartment

NEW YORK, NEW YORK

In a very different kind of Fifth Avenue apartment house—a prewar building transformed into a modern postwar one with balconies—the idea was to frame views of Central Park and the owner's collection of contemporary arts and crafts. But the frames themselves, which contain glass door panels, track lighting, built-in cabinets, even the bed, became works of art. Their burnished zinc finish (inspired by a draftsman's triangle), and visible joinery make the frames look both handmade and inserted, as all the interior casework and partitions obviously are. Display shelves and window seats are tucked into frames or niches, so that floor space is maximized and each element has its place in the whole. While creating separate, private rooms, the architects have managed to preserve the feeling of lightness and openness in this 1,800 square-foot (170-square-meter) apartment without sacrificing the human scale and delicacy that had once been there. A one-inch (2.5-cm) reveal on solid walls echoes the one-inch width of the frame; both define a six-foot-eight-inch (two-meter) datum repeated throughout the apartment on window mullions, at the top of the kitchen cabinets, and on top of the tile in the bathroom. Steps at the east end of the living area lead up to the bedroom, which has been elevated to provide a view of the park from the bed; stairs at the west end step up to a recovered porch, separated from the living room itself by full-height transparent doors that open the apartment literally and visually to the park.

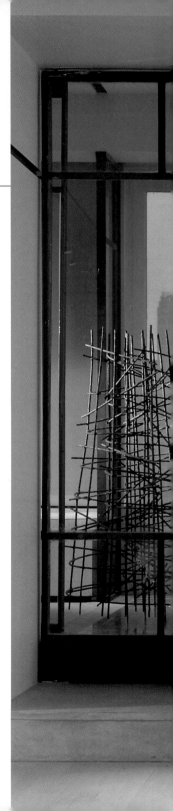

The glass-enclosed winter terrace is shared by the living room and bedroom, enlarging both and offering an expansive view of the park. On the floor, a chalky limestone band borders a pool of glistening marble tiles which reflect the view.

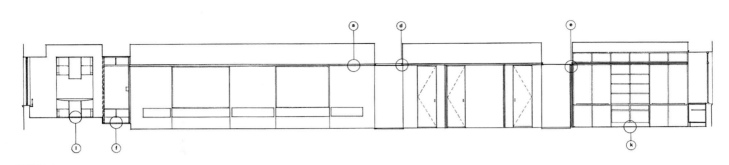

SECTION A-A

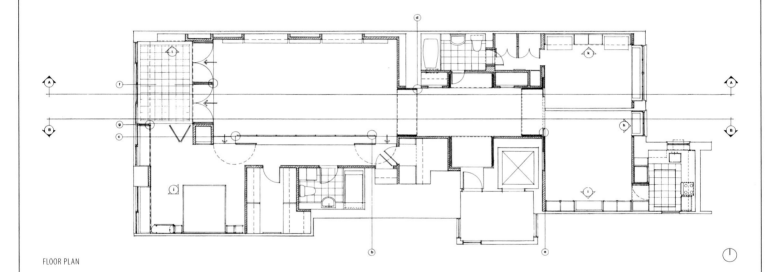

FLOOR PLAN

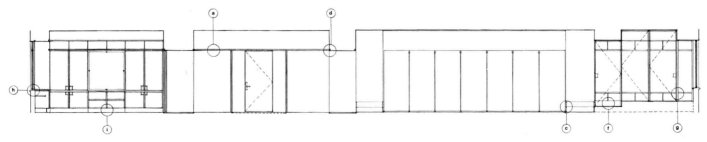

SECTION B-B

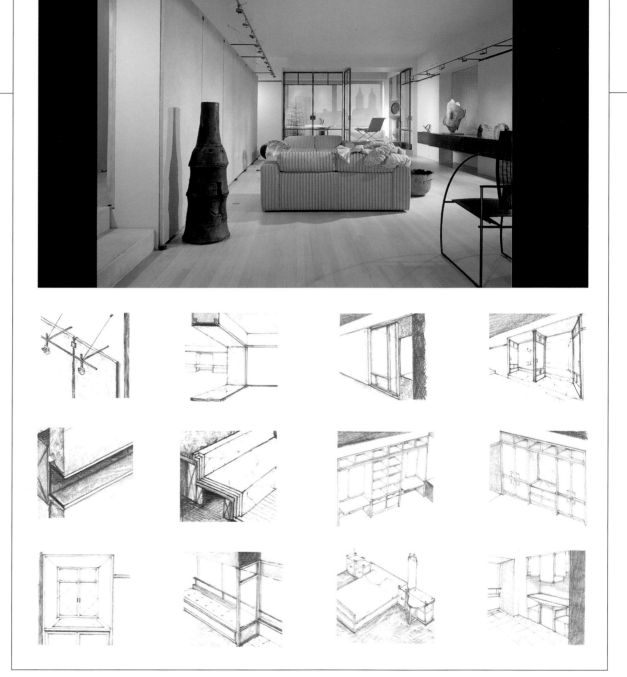

Gallery lighting, wall niches, and zinc-clad display shelves showcase works from the owner's collection, while the architectural elements' simple forms and subdued colors allow the art objects to be the focus of attention. Materials, chosen for their richness, warmth, and solidity, are limestone, zinc with a patina, sandblasted steel, ebony, oak, and marble.

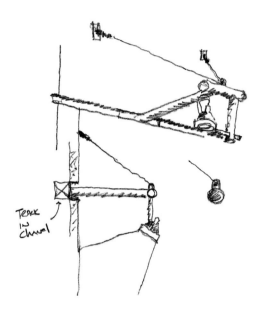

Track
in channel

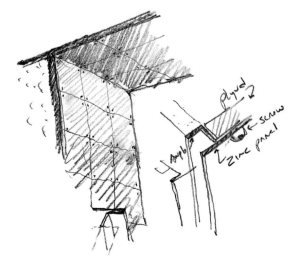

plywd

angle screw
zinc panel

Room divisions are defined by zinc-lined portals that mark passage from one room to the next, without actually closing off individual spaces. Throughout the apartment, openness and fluidity are balanced with a more traditional sense of residential intimacy and enclosure.

To the east of the entry hall are the more private and smaller dining room and den, which are lined with storage units, exhibit space, and work areas. Their design continues the datum established by the transom steel casements and maintained throughout the apartment.

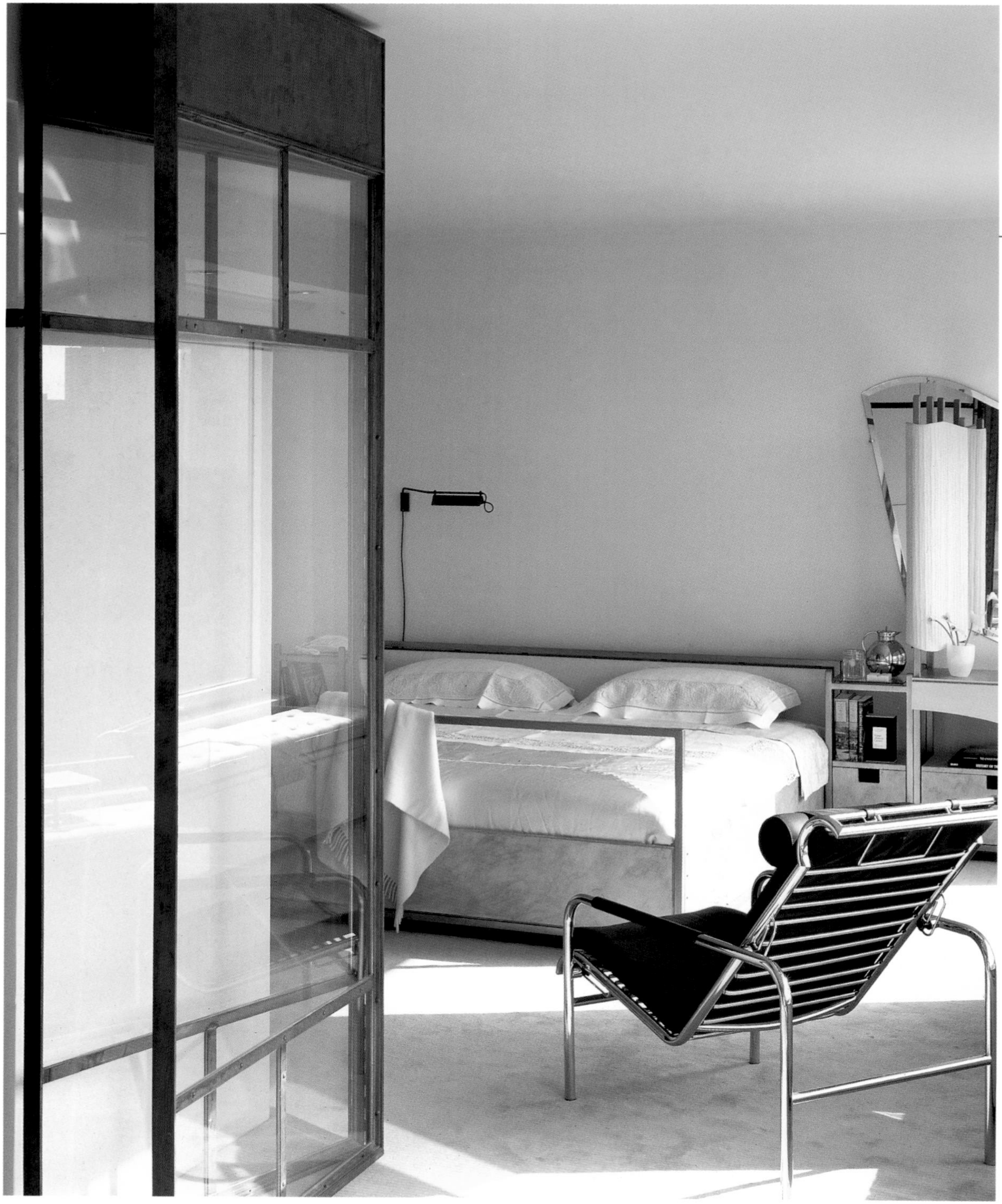

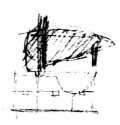

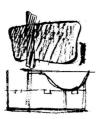

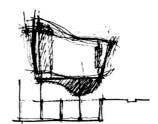

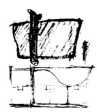

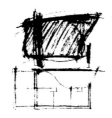

The bedroom, raised several inches from the level of the main living areas, becomes a private retreat. Bedroom elements depart from the interior's overall geometry with the introduction of softer materials and curvy, organic shapes.

Crafts Collector's Pied-à-Terre

NEW YORK, NEW YORK

The challenge of displaying a rotating collection of American crafts was considerable in this bland little postwar apartment. With only 750 square feet (70 square meters) to work with, a number of dramatic pieces of handmade furniture to accommodate, and a substantial requirement for storage space, the architects stripped the apartment back to a simple elongated box. Though they removed all the interior partitions, the architects preserved their trace with glass bricks embedded in the floor and then went to work creating new freestanding walls that house seating and cabinetry, even a small hideaway office. One wall-like storage unit separates the living room from the bedroom; another, running the length of the space, contains benches and display shelves. The one-bedroom apartment became a kind of loft—with an intimacy lofts rarely achieve. The hand-plastered finish in muted colors on the gently curving wall that screens the kitchen provides an ethereal backdrop for paintings. On the kitchen side, the space widens to become the dining area. Bleached wood floors, light wood drawers and doors, white walls, and rich textured fabrics in the same light, neutral tones create a hushed setting where the colorful, wild, and wonderful collections can stand out under artfully controlled lighting from rows of custom-crafted metal fixtures that crane over partitions to spotlight specific objects, from ceiling canisters that warm and brighten the entire space, and, concealed in the casework, from fixtures whose light washes up and down simultaneously.

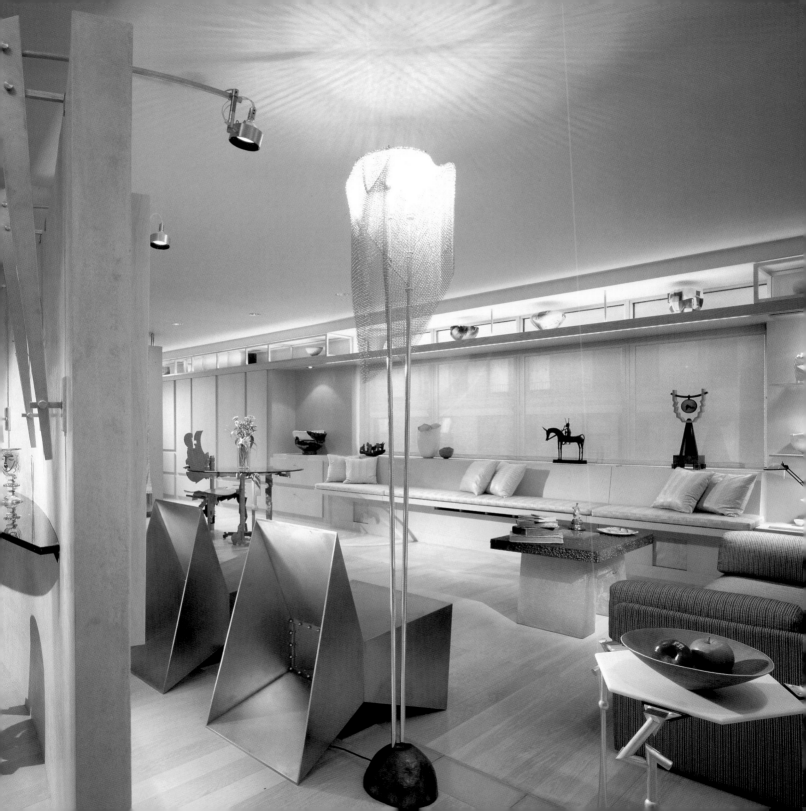

FLOOR PLAN

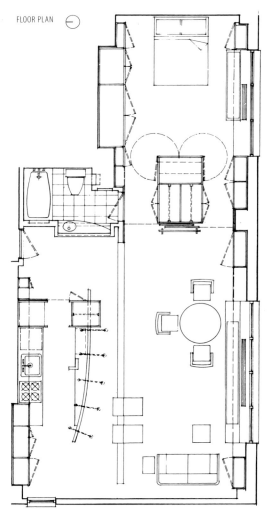

The free-standing, curved wall that sets off the kitchen is capped with custom-designed light fixtures that teeter above, providing work light in the kitchen and art lighting for the living room. The open floor plan provides breathing space in confined quarters for the client's collection of sculpted craft furniture.

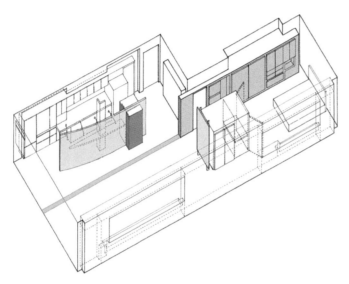

To achieve a long perspective, the architects reconstructed the window wall as a continuous wood ensemble which houses display, storage, and seating. As the unit passes from living space to the sleeping area, it reveals the client's extensive collection in a series of niches, shelves, and ledges with concealed lighting that accentuates the objects.

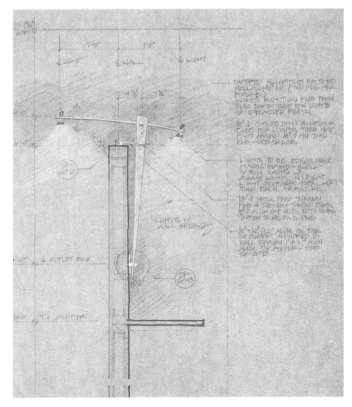
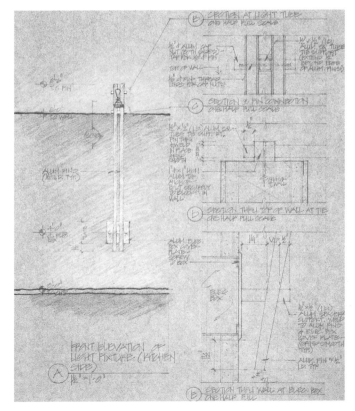

Fifth Avenue Apartment

NEW YORK, NEW YORK

The contrast between the dramatic way the architects approached this apartment and the way they designed another one with a Secessionist salon ten years earlier, in the same building on a lower floor, demonstrates how they respond to contexts established by different collections. Here, they used strong architectural moves, instead of subtle gestures, to situate bold modern art and African sculpture in a domestic setting without overpowering the sense of a home or turning the art into decoration. Large wood wall panels, pedestals, niches, and juxtaposed horizontal and vertical planes provide the works of art with environments of their own. Heavy furnishings and rich materials, like the striated planar marble mantle and the polished African mahogany floors, provide counterpoint to the powerful objects, as do angled, cushioned window seats framed by the lightly draped sheer fabric panels—almost curtains. Pocket doors made of a silk and steel fabric form a translucent scrim between the living and dining rooms. Even the kitchen has paneling in fine woods, marble backsplashes, and a handsomely patterned wood floor, all in the same palette of white, off white, yellowy wood, and dark gray used throughout the apartment. A knife-edge picture railing on the same module as the reveal above the panels also runs throughout, ordering the whole. It establishes a scale appropriate both to the works of art and to the generous traditional prewar room plan, with the master bedroom overlooking Central Park.

Deep thresholds emphasize transition from one space to the next and give a sense of traditional rooms to what is in reality a series of spaces that open onto one another. The thresholds are lined with rich materials and at key moments contain display niches and shelves for the owner's collection.

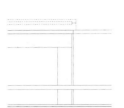
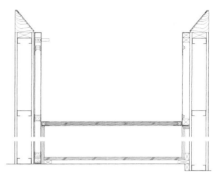

FIREPLACE SCREEN DETAIL

DISPLAY NICHE

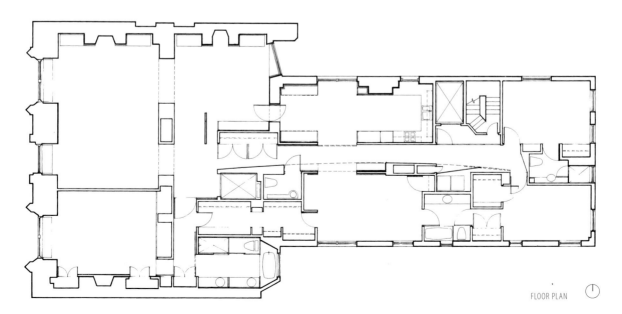

FLOOR PLAN

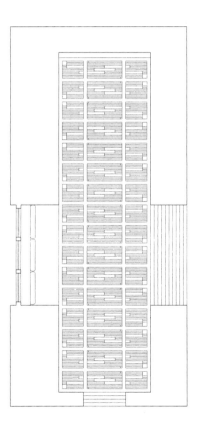

The owner's evolving art collection is accommodated by a modern interpretation of the traditional picture molding: a steel plate that passes through the apartment's walls and extends just an inch and a half into the room. At each threshold, its full width is expressed. Small holes incised in the steel at regular intervals are threaded with airplane wire to hang the collection.

KITCHEN FLOOR PATTERN

Prasada Apartment

Since most of the walls in this turn-of-the-century apartment with a typical Victorian plan had been removed previously, creating an amorphous, loft-like space, the architects decided to restore the order of the original plan of a corridor between the service rooms and living spaces without putting back all the partitions that divided the public spaces into separate little chambers. They created an elliptical foyer to provide a sense of entry and reestablished the hall by means of a series of structural columns, stripped to the bone, and a 35-foot- (11-meter-) long floating canopy with lights washing the ceiling and spotlighting the ebony-stained wood floor. The living room, dining area, and den off to one side all have views of Central Park through the colonnade on the corridor promenade.

The rooms in the 3,200-square-foot (300-square-meter), two-bedroom apartment are spacious enough to give this collection of recent American art room to breathe—even though the artwork required several different settings: monochromatic paintings by Ad Reinhardt and Sam Revelas required quiet backgrounds; more energetic works by Frank Stella, Susan Rothenberg, Jonathan Borofsky, and Willem de Kooning needed walls of their own; and large African statues had to be tucked into niches. Geometric details—tight rows of lights, unadorned windows, a black lacquered door frame, and pocket doors between the dining area and the den—create an overarching setting and bring order to the apartment as a whole.

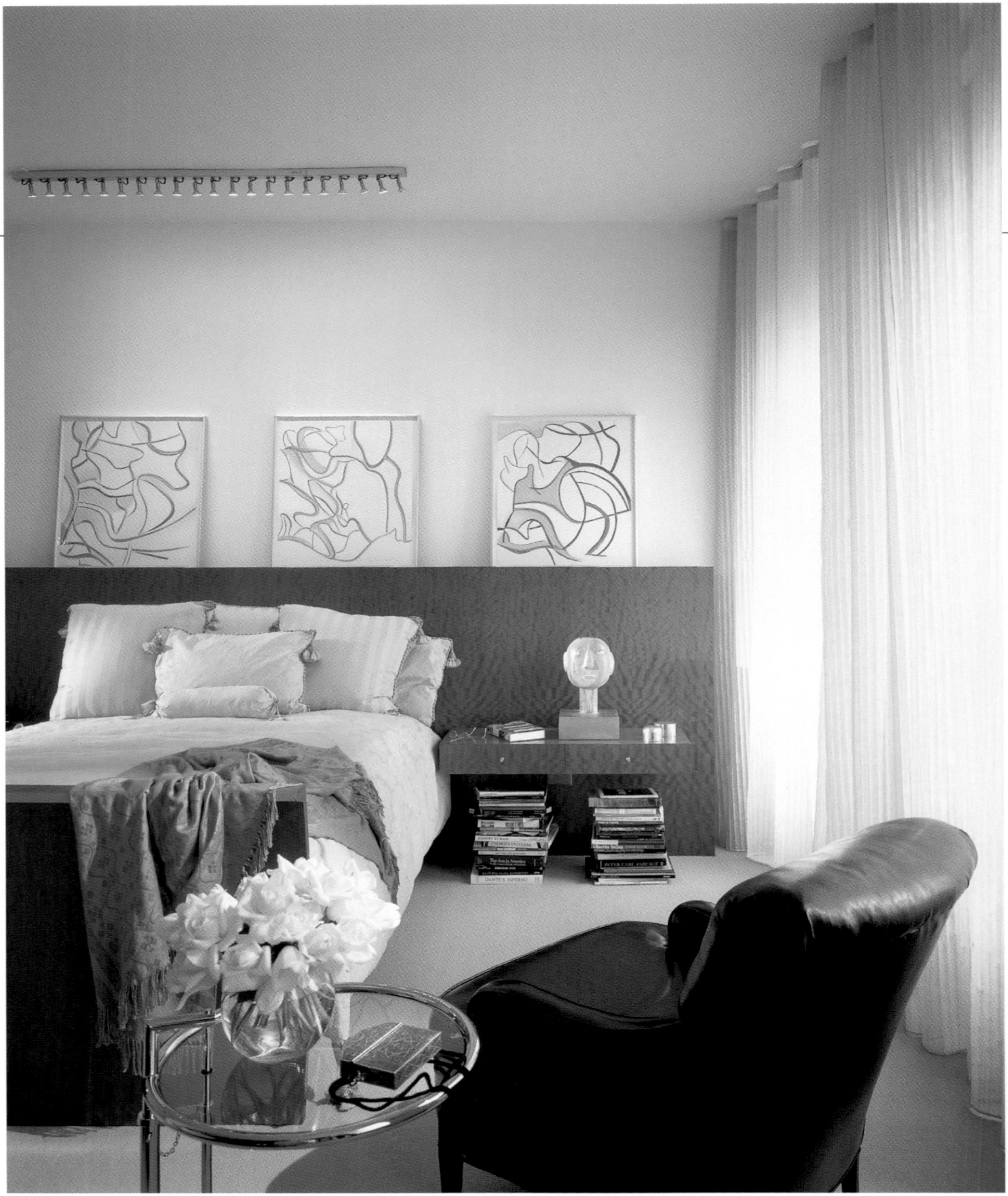

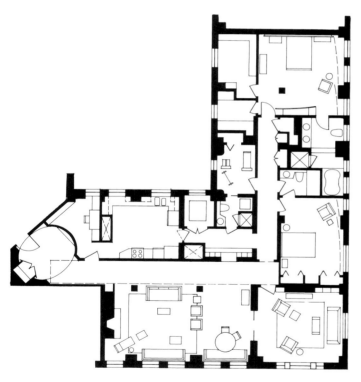

FLOOR PLAN

0   5'   10'

The furnishings are a collection of classic modern pieces, mixing Arts & Crafts with Art Deco and contemporary objects. The headboard of the custom-designed bed casually displays the client's artwork, while providing bedside storage and controls for the lighting, audio system and draperies.

Bachelor's Downtown Loft

The master suite on the lower level of this duplex apartment in an old commercial building has an atmosphere of luxurious, quiet refinement. Translucent glass panels set in crisp white frames divide the space into a separate bedroom, den, and workout room that becomes guest quarters when desired. The furniture is framed in bronze, made of rich teak, and covered with light textured fabrics. A broad row of picture windows overlooks the green oval of Madison Square Park, but there are touches of drama: Napoleon LeBrun's Metropolitan Life tower (the Saint Mark's campanile grown to 700 feet/213 meters) and its gigantic, colored clock looms in the foreground. A polished bronze pole with a delicate glass shelf pivots a wall-sized mirror around the bed. And veils of light created by a complex and changeable system turn the entire apartment into a slightly surreal but very restrained casbah.

But in the bathroom, nothing is restrained. Colored steam rises from a Jacuzzi bubbling to a syncopated beat (it can be timed to music) and a rainbow of reflections bounces off handmade glass lamps attached to the back-painted glass walls by bronze brackets and burning aromatic oils. The shower-for-two is as big as most New York kitchens. Other bathroom walls are covered with platinum leaf. Fiber-optic lighting tints the bath water and Jacuzzi jets an intense range of hues.

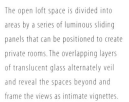

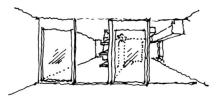

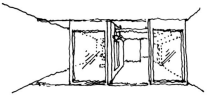

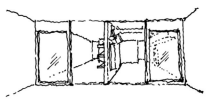

The open loft space is divided into areas by a series of luminous sliding panels that can be positioned to create private rooms. The overlapping layers of translucent glass alternately veil and reveal the spaces beyond and frame the views as intimate vignettes.

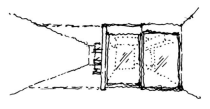

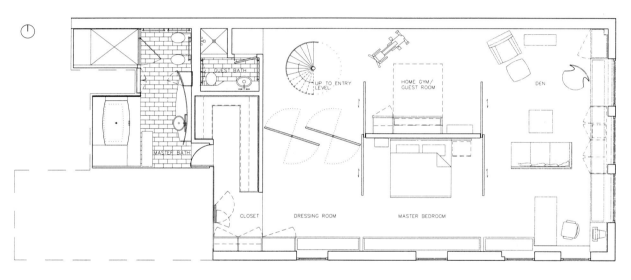

The color palette is restricted, but the selection of materials is not. Textures range from shimmering back-painted glass to rough-hewn teak. The lighting system showcases the furnishings and transforms the glass panels into theatrical scrims, changing them from transparent to opaque.

The Root House

Inside an existing shell of fluted concrete block, the architects created an independent interior architecture of freestanding slabs, curved planes, suspended panels, mesh screens, and cable railings, set apart from the outside walls, to define the activity areas and passageways. They decided to make visually explicit the distinction between their own light planar insertions, which are sculptural elements in their own right, and the rough, earthbound outer walls that had been built by another architect, William Morgan of Florida. A thin wooden bridge, hung by cables from a tall notched aluminum tower on one side of the U-shaped structure, connects it with a copper mesh tower that screens the main public rooms on the other, penetrating a three-story atrium that serves as the dining room and main entertaining space. A wing-like curved wooden plane floats over the living room like a second ceiling; the fireplace wall is a freestanding arc of maple burl which sweeps away from the outer wall. The light, planar elements, which reveal glimpses of the spaces they demarcate, bring human scale to a grand space within the 8,500-square-foot (790-square-meter) interior.

Despite the use of heavy materials such as Idaho stone and an onyx shower wall in the bath, the interior effect is of weightlessness and suspension because the masonry exterior cuts off views of nearby dwellings.

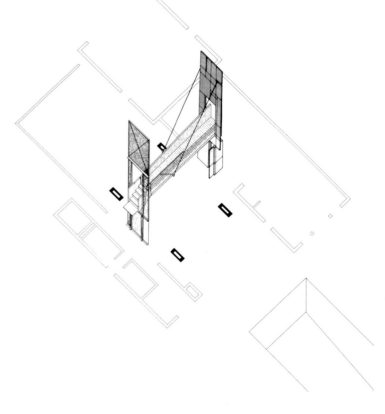

Fully glazed on one side, the triple-volume refectory is an extension of the ocean into the house. The cantilevered beechwood bridge mediates between the refectory's grand scale and the more intimate proportions of the living areas that flank it.

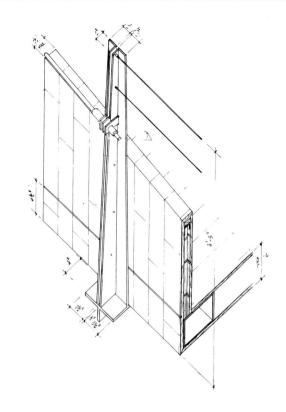

THIRD FLOOR PLAN

1. PRIVATE OFFICE
2. CLOSET
3. WALK-IN CLOSET
4. MASTER BATHROOM
5. MASTER BEDROOM
6. RAMP
7. GALLERY BELOW
8. OBSERVATION DECK

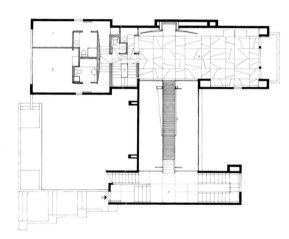

SECOND FLOOR PLAN

1. MAID'S ROOM
2. GUEST ROOM
3. PRIVATE STAIR
4. LIBRARY
5. BRIDGE
6. ENTRY
7. FOYER

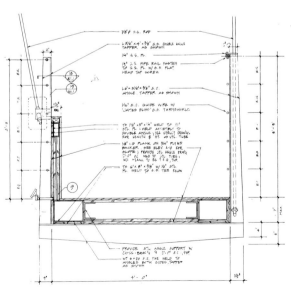

FIRST FLOOR PLAN

1. GARAGE
2. PANTRY
3. PRIVATE STAIR
4. KITCHEN
5. LIVING ROOM
6. GARDEN
7. GALLERY
8. CHANGING ROOM

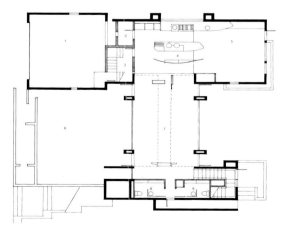

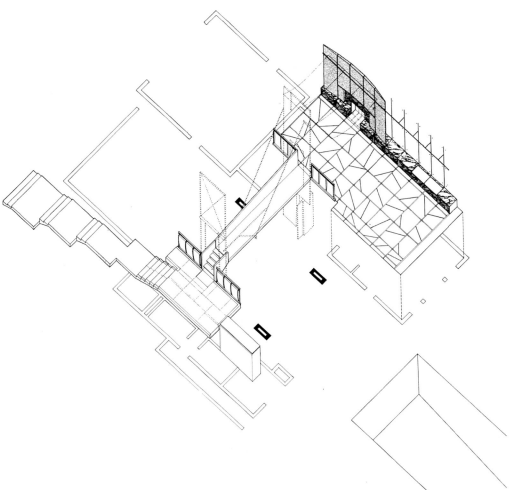

Redefining the character of the living room space that fills most of the second floor, the room's back wall stands free of the house's shell, and an ashwood canopy floats above. The floor comprises cherry planks framed with ebony in a modified grid.

A thin, bowed maple panel traces the boundary between the single-story kitchen and the massive refectory. The screen encloses the kitchen on one axis, while leaving it open on the other to look out toward the ocean. At the heart of the kitchen, an antique teak countertop rests on a concrete base inset with glass blocks. As the base was being cast onsite, the architects mixed colored and metallic powders into the concrete to enliven its surface.

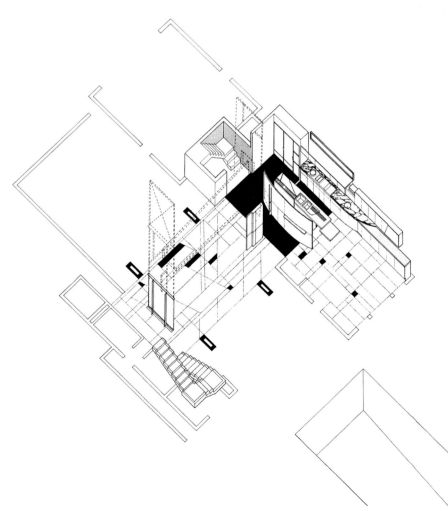

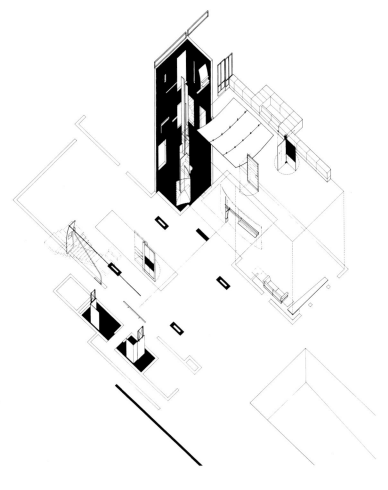

A light metal stair connects the north section's three floors. As it reaches the third level, its cherry wood rail engages a sculptural magazine rack of stainless steel panels and wire mesh. Continuing the interplay among contrasting materials that resonates throughout the house, these elements face the translucent brass-framed onyx wall that encloses the master bath.

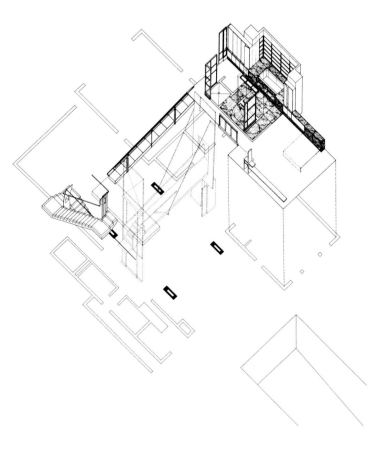

The third floor, with bedrooms, bathrooms, office, and study, is the owner's sanctuary. Disparate materials-some left raw, others refined-are brought together in carefully crafted architectural details.

Appendix ▶

Selected Buildings

1998–present
Congregation Rodeph Sholom
New York, New York

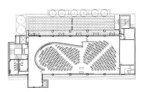  

1996–present
Triple Bridges
Port Authority of New York and New Jersey
New York, New York

1994–97
Columbia University Graduate School
of Journalism
New York, New York

1990–93
TransResources, Inc.
Office Interior Renovation
New York, New York

1990–92
Columbia Presbyterian Medical Center
Division of Cardiothoracic Surgery
New York, New York

1990–91
Allegheny College Housing
Meadville, Pennsylvania

 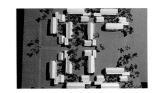 

1988–89
Joseph E. Seagram & Sons, Inc.
New York, New York

1987–91
Physics Building Addition
University of Virginia
Charlottesville, Virginia

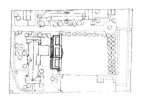  

1988–91
Chemical Engineering & Research Building
University of Virginia
Charlottesville, Virginia

1987–88
Bill Blass, Ltd.
New York, New York
(Wayne Berg with Richard Weinstein)

PROJECTS AND ONGOING WORKS

1986–87
Anne Klein Co.
New York, New York
(Wayne Berg with Richard Weinstein)

1986
McLarnon-Zingesser House
Fishers Island, New York
(Wayne Berg with Richard Weinstein)

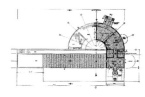  

1983–87
Collector's Apartment
New York, New York

1982–84
Gallatin County Detention Center
Bozeman, Montana
(Wayne Berg with Ozzie Berg, BGS Architects)

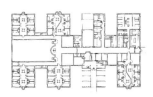  

1981–82
Doig House
White Sulphur Springs, Montana
(Wayne Berg with Ozzie Berg, BGS Architects)

1979–84
George & Annette Murphy Center
at Asphalt Green
New York, New York

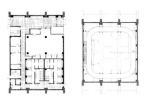  

1979–83
Joseph E. Seagram & Sons, Inc.
Aircraft Hangar, Laboratories, & Offices
Purchase, New York

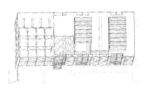  

1978–82
Field House and Ice Hockey Rink
Fredonia, New York

1976–81
Columbia Grammar & Preparatory School
New York, New York

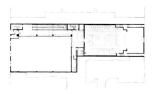  

1976–82
Little Italy Housing
New York, New York

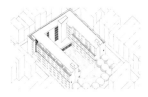  

PROJECTS AND ONGOING WORKS

1976
Powell Condominiums
Powell, Wyoming
(Wayne Berg with Ozzie Berg, BGS Architects)

1976–present
Ongoing Curatorship of the Seagram Building
New York, New York

1974–75
Wine Museum
Joseph E. Seagram & Sons, Inc.
New York, New York

1973–75
Joseph E. Seagram & Sons, Inc.
Des Plaines, Illinois
(Giovanni Pasanella Architect)

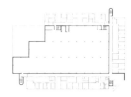

1969–73; 1970–74
Twin Parks West Housing,
Twin Parks East Housing
Bronx, New York
(Giovanni Pasanella Architect)

1969–71
Administration Tower
State University College at Potsdam, New York
(Giovanni Pasanella Architect)

1969–73
New York City Fire Department
Firehouse and Chief's Headquarters
Brooklyn, New York
(Giovanni Pasanella Architect)

1969
Brown House
Ringoes, New Jersey
(Giovanni Pasanella Architect)

1968
Dunbar House
Winhall, Vermont
(Giovanni Pasanella Architect)

1967
Grey House
Wellfleet, Massachusetts

List of Works and Credits

REED LIBRARY ADDITION AND RENOVATION
State University College at Fredonia
Fredonia, New York, 1986–94
Award:1995 AIA New York State Association of Architects Design Excellence Award
Client: New York State University Construction Fund
Project Team: Wayne Berg, J. Arvid Klein, Lea H. Cloud: John Adams, Oswald Berg, Nancy Cooper, Vivian Ditischein, Gabriel Frenandez, Ed Harter, Betty Liu, Shelley Martin, Victoria Rospond, Harley Swedler, Nader Tehrani
Structural Engineer: Syracuse Engineers
Mechanical Engineer: Babinsky-Klein Engineering, P.C.
Library Consultant: Ellsworth Mason, Ph.D.
Lighting Consultant: Kugler Tillotson Associates, Inc.
Contractor: Whipple Allen Construction Co. (Phase I), L.G. Hall Contractor, Inc. (Phase II)
Photographers: Paul Warchol (with small detail shots by Wayne Berg)

EDUCATION AND DEVELOPMENT CENTER
Clinch Valley College of the University of Virginia
Wise, Virginia, 1993–97
Awards: 1995 Progressive Architecture P/A Awards Citation; 1994 AIA New York City Design Award
Client: University of Virginia
Project Team: Wayne Berg, Albert Ho, Jonathan R. Knowles, Lawrence Zeroth
Associate Architect: Balzer and Associates, Roanoke, Virginia
Structural Engineer: Dunbar Milby & Williams
Mechanical Engineer: Whitescarver, Hurd, Obenchain
Photographer: Jock Pottle/Esto

STABILE HALL DORMITORY
Pratt Institute
Brooklyn, New York, 1997–2000
Award: 1997 AIA New York City Design Award
Client: Pratt Institute
Project Team: Wayne Berg, John C. Kelleher, Timothy Archambault, Melissa Atherley, Howard Chu, Don Keppler, Taiji Miyasaka, Jonathan Schecter, Christine Wentz
Competition: See Yuen Chuang, Oliviero Godi, Tim Witzig, Kwong Yung Yu, Michael Yung
Landscape Architect: Signe Nielsen, P.C.
Structural Engineer: Tor, Smolen, Calini & Anastos
Mechanical Engineer: Goldman Copeland Associates
Lighting Consultant: Kugler Tillotson Associates, Inc.
Photographer: Jock Pottle/Esto

WORLD WAR II MEMORIAL
Competition for Memorial on Washington Mall
Washington, D.C., 1997
Competition Sponsor: National Battle Monuments Commission
Design Team: Wayne Berg, Albert Ho, Howard Chu
Photographer: Jock Pottle/Esto

WILLIAMSBURG COMMUNITY CENTER
Williamsburg Houses
Brooklyn, New York, 1997–99
Client: New York City Housing Authority
Project Team: Wayne Berg, Lawrence Zeroth, Melissa Atherley, Howard Chu, John C. Kelleher, Taiji Miyasaka
Competition: Kwong Yung Yu, Michael Yung
Structural Engineer: LeRoy Callender P.C.
Mechanical Engineer: Goldman Copeland Associates, P.C.
Landscape Architect: Signe Nielsen, P.C.
Lighting Consultant: Kugler Tillotson Associates, Inc.
Photographer: Jock Pottle/Esto

PRIMARY AND INTERMEDIATE SCHOOL 89M
Battery Park City, New York, New York
Project Team: Pasanella + Klein Stolzman + Berg Architects, P.C.
Wayne Berg, Henry Stolzman, Jonathan R. Knowles, Lea H. Cloud, Christine Wentz, Costas Kondylis & Associates Richard Cook & Associates
Structural Engineer: Ysrael Seinuck, P.C.
Mechanical/Electrical Engineer: Cosentini Associates
Acoustical Consultant: Cerami & Associates, Inc.
Lighting Consultant: Kugler Tillotsen Associates, Inc.
Construction Manager: Lehrer McGovern Bovis, Inc.
Photographers: Paul Warchol, Kentaro Tsubaki (photograph of hallway gathering area at dusk)

THE SHOREHAM HOTEL
New York, New York, 1993–95
Client: Gotham Hospitality Group
Project Team: Henry Stolzman, Wayne Berg, Tim Witzig, Jonathan Schecter
Lighting Consultant: Johnson/Schwinghammer
Contractor: Vanguard Construction & Development Co., Inc.
Photographer: Chuck Choi

THE FRANKLIN HOTEL
New York, New York, 1992–94
Client: Gotham Hospitality Group
Project Team: Henry Stolzman, Wayne Berg, Tim Witzig, Jonathan Schecter, Albert Ho, John C. Kelleher
Lighting Consultant: Johnson/Schwinghammer
Contractor: Gotham Hospitality Group
Photographer: Chuck Choi

THE MANSFIELD HOTEL
New York, New York, 1994–96
Awards: 1996 Interior Magazine Annual Award (Best Hotel)
Client: Gotham Hospitality Group
Project Team: Henry Stolzman, Wayne Berg, Tim Witzig, Jonathan Schecter, Howard Chu
Lighting Consultant: Johnson/Schwinghammer
Contractor: Gotham Hospitality Group
Photographers: Michael Moran (pages 76, 77, 79);
and Simon Watson (pages 75, 78, 80, 81)

ART COLLECTOR'S APARTMENT
New York, New York, 1986–89
Awards: 1989 AIA New York State Award for Excellence in Design;
1989 AIA New York City Design Award
Project Team: Wayne Berg, Henry Stolzman, Giovanni Pasanella, Lea H. Cloud, Nancy Cooper, Harley Swedler
Interior Consultant: Tse-Yun Chu Studio
Lighting Consultant: Kugler Tillotson Associates, Inc.
Mechanical Engineer: Jack Green Associates
Photographers: Paul Warchol and John Hall (pages 96 and 97, middle)

CRAFTS COLLECTOR'S PIED-À-TERRE
New York, New York, 1989–91
Client: Name Withheld
Project Team: Wayne Berg, Henry Stolzman, Lea H. Cloud, Janet Roseff
Interior Consultant: Tse-Yun Chu Studio
Lighting Consultant: Kugler Tillotson Associates, Inc.
Photographer: Chuck Choi

FIFTH AVENUE APARTMENT
New York, New York, 1990–93
Project Team: Henry Stolzman, Wayne Berg, Lea H. Cloud, Jonathan Schecter, Albert Ho, Elyse Jane Ostland, John C. Kelleher, Betty Liu, Emily Moss, Janet Roseff, Tim Witzig
Interior Consultant: Tse-Yun Chu Studio
Lighting Consultant: Johnson/Schwinghammer
Contractor: R.C. Dolner, Inc.
Photographer: Paul Warchol

PRASADA APARTMENT
New York, New York, 1992–94
Project Team: Henry Stolzman, Wayne Berg, Jonathan Schecter
Lighting Consultant: Johnson Schwinghammer
Contractor: Massartre, Ltd.
Photographer: Chuck Choi

BACHELOR'S DOWNTOWN LOFT
New York, New York, 1995–97
Client: Name Withheld
Project Team: Henry Stolzman, Lea H. Cloud, Jonathan Schecter, Troy Ostrander
Lighting Consultant: Johnson/Schwinghammer
Contractor: Vanguard Construction & Development Co., Inc.
Photographer: Paul Warchol

THE ROOT HOUSE
Ormond Beach, Florida, 1990–95
Awards: 1996 AIA National Honor Award; 1995 AIA New York State Association of Architects Design Excellence Award; 1995 AIA New York Chapter Design Award
Client: Chapman Root II
Project Team: Wayne Berg, Albert Ho, Natalie Bailey, Elyse Jane Ostland, Su Kim, John Stuart
Interior Consultant: Tse Yun Chu Studio
Lighting Consultant: Kugler Tillotson Associates, Inc.
Contractor: The Root Company
Photographers: Paul Warchol (with small detail shots by Wayne Berg)

Pasanella+Klein Stolzman+Berg Architects, P.C., from left to right (above): John C. Kelleher, Kentaro Tsubaki, Henry Stolzman, Tim Witzig, Lawrence Zeroth, Taiji Miyasaka, J. Arvid Klein, Jonathan Schecter, Tony McAndrew, Judy Fogel, Howard Chu, Wayne Berg, Nina Seirafi, Christine Wentz, Timothy Archambault, Ron Rubenstein, and Don Keppler.

ACKNOWLEDGMENTS

Although architectural concept books are common, this book, like our practice, is about realized (or about-to-be realized) buildings. There would be no buildings without clients, and there can be no good or exceptional ones without extraordinary clients whose vision, patience, and sustained commitment make it possible to develop ideas and translate them into form.

Without our unusually talented staff, whose dedication, hard work, and critical contributions made our buildings what they became, this book would not have taken the shape it has.

Without Jennifer Harris, there would be no book. Her encouragement and effort made it possible for the authors to bring it to completion, and her critical eye contributed in no small measure to its clarity and content.

And without Paul Warchol, Chuck Choi, and Jock Pottle, whose photographs have consistently captured the essence of our work, it would have been impossible to bring it to the page.